The Best Walks and Trails in NSW

The Best
WALKS & TRAILS
in NSW

Sean and Melanie Greenhill

NH
NEW
HOLLAND

Acknowledgement

In the writing of this book, we are aware of the cultural significance and connection that the traditional custodians have to country. We would like to acknowledge those Traditional Custodians of Country throughout New South Wales – those who walked these lands for thousands of years before European settlement. We aspire in our writing to impart appreciation for country as held by the traditional custodians. We pay our respects to Elders past and present.

Introduction

With over 900 reserves under National Parks and Wildlife Service management and uncounted tracks, trails and reserves under local management, New South Wales presents a world of diverse and intriguing walking opportunities. In this book we have aimed to capture the diversity of the walks on offer, including walks of cultural significance, walks that showcase the diversity of landscapes, vegetation, wildlife, birdlife and experience on offer in New South Wales.

We have included walks with some history, culture or further interest points attached and provided some insight into these aspects of the walk. Too often we have finished a walk, only to realise we have missed an important

aspect of what the location had to offer. Having said that, we realise that the book has to have limits and so we have kept things as succinct as possible.

The directions included for these walks are only a guide. Where a walk has less signage, there will be more in the description to keep you on track. Where the walk is clearly signposted, the directions will be a very simple guide of what to expect.

The focus is on walks of 2–3 hours in duration. Keep in mind some walks may take longer if you stop to swim, gaze at whales, bird watch, read the information boards or just picnic at a good vantage spot along the way – all of which we highly recommend.

The walks we chose to write about can be achieved with average fitness, and we have included a few more challenging walks that can be tackled after some more experience on the trails. Each walk is graded, indicating the level of difficulty.

The grading system used is the Australian Walking Track Grading System (AWTGS –see page 10). This system has been devised by the National Parks and Wildlife Service of New South Wales and is the gold standard for track grading. Tracks are graded from 1 to 5 and the grading process takes into account factors such as experience required, steps, gradient, path quality and signage. Each track is graded on the most difficult of these criteria rather than the average. This means that a grade 3 walk, will *at its most difficult*, meet the grade 3 criteria and could very well be graded at 2 or even 1 in certain sections.

Prior to starting a walk, it is wise to consider your abilities and limitations and pick walks that are well within your capabilities to ensure an enjoyable and safe experience. In addition to the grade, we have included trail quality for each walk. This indicates whether there are steps, steep sections, rock scrambling and whether the track is signposted. This information should help you make an informed decision on which walks to set out on. Further to this information some research into the weather events from previous weeks, as well as forecast weather for the day of your walk, is pertinent information to consider. The Bureau of Meteorology (http://www.bom. gov.au) or Weatherzone (https://www.weatherzone.com.au) websites are both reliable sources for weather information. National Parks and Wildlife Service include alerts on their website (https://www.nationalparks.nsw.gov. au) for each of their reserves which indicate whether trails are closed or damaged. Unfortunately, day-by-day information on the condition of tracks in locally managed parks and reserves is not centralised.

What to take along on a walk is aways an interesting discussion. The rule of thumb is to include things you might need – within reason – while considering the following: the terrain of the walk, the duration of the walk, weather patterns for the area, what you would need to sustain yourself if you were to need to be rescued, contingencies for other risks.

The more difficult the terrain, the higher the risk of a slip, fall or accident. Considering the terrain, also consider shoe choice and carrying a first aid kit to be able to patch yourself up if required.

A rescue in a remote area can take hours, *if not a full day to complete*. Not only do services need to be summoned, but they also need to travel to the closest access point and then make their way to you, often on foot. Considering this, we recommend a space blanket, a snakebite bandage, reserves of food and water and clothing to rug up and stave off shock symptoms. Consider what you need to sustain yourself while awaiting rescue – again, this depends on how long it might be for rescue services to get to you.

Weather patterns for the specific area you are walking in hugely impact what gear you will need to take along. Weather changes quickly in alpine areas and on mountain tops and afternoon storms are not uncommon in coastal regions. A rain jacket, several thermals, gloves, beanie or buff and dry socks are all essential when walking in alpine areas. Hat, wind jacket, sunscreen and water for hotter and more exposed areas. *Insect repellent is a must for wet landscapes.* All these items can be rolled up and carried in a backpack. On Page 8 there is a comprehensive list of gear to consider for your walk.

Our thoughts are that if you get to the end of your walk and have not needed any of your safety gear, it's been a great walk! The other thing to consider is that the people who come to our assistance if we need a rescue, often put their own lives at risk by coming to our aid. The least we can do is be prepared *to help ourselves* as much as is reasonable.

The walks listed take place in a mix of National Parks and in locally managed reserves. Bear in mind that some National Parks charge fees for entry or for parking. These fees go towards NPWS' conservation and maintenance budgets, so we consider these fees well spent. There are also annual Parks Passes available for purchase that allow access to multiple National Parks for a year, which might prove to be more efficient than paying a fee every time a Park is used (https://www.nationalparks.nsw.gov.au/passes-and-fees/annual-passes).

The diversity of walking experiences in New South Wales is truly exciting and as walkers we appreciate the work of the National Parks and Wildlife Service in keeping the trails maintained and safe. Further the councils and other governing bodies that add to and maintain the body of trails in New South Wales should also be commended for their work in offering some great natural experiences for walkers.

Australian Walking Track Grading System (AWTGS)

A walk of a certain grade might include, *at its most difficult section*, some or all the following characteristics.

Grade 1

- No bushwalking experience required
- Flat, even surface
- No steps or steep sections
- Not greater than 5 km in total length
- Suitable for wheelchair users with a person to assist

Grade 2

- No bushwalking experience required
- Hardened or compacted surface
- Gentle hills or occasional steps
- No greater than 10 km in total length

Grade 3

- Some bushwalking experience recommended
- Could have rough surface
- Steep hills or many steps
- Up to 20 km in total length

Grade 4

- Bushwalking experience recommended
- Rough surfaces
- Long, rough or very steep hills or steps
- Limited directional signage
- Might be more than 20 km in total length

Grade 5

- Very experienced bushwalkers with specialised skills including navigation and emergency first aid
- Rough tracks
- Very steep hills or many steps
- Unmarked trails
- Might be more than 20 km in total length

Gear List for Consideration

Weather forecasts and temperature and rainfall averages for the area you are walking in should be considered before starting out. Weather changes quickly in mountain areas and coastal walks often don't have much cover to shelter from summer storms. Higher areas compel you to take warm and waterproof coverings and on a coastal walk you should be prepared for sun, wind and heat. *Insect repellent is a must for wet landscapes*, for bugs and also for leeches. Also recommended:

- Beanie
- Gaiters
- Buff
- Gloves
- Hat
- Thermal
- Wind Jacket
- Rain Jacket
- Fleece
- Spare socks
- Good shoes – Whether you use hiking boots or trail running shoes is often a matter of personal preference. Rockier and wetter walks will require shoes with more grip on their tread, whereas some can be walked in any type of running shoe.

Food:

- You should have enough food to keep you fuelled for the planned duration of the walk, plus for an extra couple of hours in case plans change or unexpected things happen. Consider the weight of the food you will carry. Food bars, for example, tend to be more energy dense than fruit..

Water:

- You'll need *at least 600ml for every hour on the track.* Increase this to 1 litre in hot summer weather.

Safety Equipment:

- Mobile Phone equipped with full battery life, a spare external phone battery, and the Emergency Plus App (https://www.emergencyplus.com.au). In remote areas, Telstra easily has the best phone coverage of all the mobile networks.
- Space Blanket
- Snake Bite Bandage
- Small First Aid Kit
- Blister care kit
- Whistle
- Sunscreen
- Insect repellent

Sydney Metropolitan

Central Coast and Hunter Valley

Blue Mountains

Central West

South East

Southern

North East

North West

West and Outback

Sydney Metropolitan

Minerva Pool Walking Track

A great walk to some culturally significant and magnificent rock pools in the Dharawal National Park. Minerva pool walking track passes through bushland of Sydney Golden Wattle and Mountain Devil Shrub before arriving at a lookout over the Minerva Pools. The end of the trail features Minerva Pool with pristine waters that features a rock island in the middle and is an idyllic swimming hole surrounded by bushland. **Visitors are asked to respect this is a sacred women's place for the Dharawal people and that only women and children enter the water at Minerva pool.**

Description: Walk down to the picnic area and amenities, and the track head starts opposite. Minerva Pool walking track makes its way first along a dirt road before you come to a junction which is signposted Minerva Pools to the left. Here the trail narrows and makes its way through stunning bushland. This is the country of traditional custodians, the Aboriginal Dharawal People. The track in this section can be rough under foot.

Prior to the pools, there is a small detour to the Minerva Pool Lookout. The lookout has a proper viewing area and gazes down on the picturesque pool. It is a great place to watch the pristine waters spill over the waterfall and into the pool below. The large and oddly shaped stone island sits curiously in the middle of the pool.

Leaving the lookout, return to the track and continue on to Minerva Pools. The official track ends at the top of the small waterfall. From here if you want to make your way down to the rock ledges to enjoy a picnic or rest, you will need to make your own path along the rocks.

Closest Suburb: Wedderburn, Campbelltown.

Start Location: Carpark at the locked gate at the end of Victoria Road, Wedderburn, near number 124 Victoria Rd.

Latitude and longitude: 34.158409°S, 150.829672°E

Grade: 3

Trail Quality: Formed trail, some steps, steep inclines in places. Clearly signed.

Distance: 2.4 km

Time: 2 hours

Amenities: At the trackhead, down from the carpark.

Park Type: Dharawal National Park

Retrace your steps back along Minerva Pool Walking Track to end of the walk on Victoria Road.

Along the Way:

Minerva Pool is a culturally significant and sacred women's place for the Dharawal people. Out of respect for the traditional owners of the land, and in further respecting the cultural importance of this site, **it is requested by the Tharawal Local Aboriginal Land Council that only women and children enter the water at Minerva Pool**.

Home to Swamp Wallabies and Yellow-Tailed Black Cockatoos, the chances of spotting these creatures are good in Dharawal National Park.

Jibbon Loop Walk

Steeped in natural beauty and aboriginal culture, Jibbon Beach, a gem in Port Hackings crown, is the centre of this walk. Starting along the streets of Bundeena, walkers make their way along Jibbon Beach and further to Jibbon Head. At the northern end of Jibbon Beach is a track leading to an Aboriginal Engraving site. The Dharawal people once lived on this land and there is a large rock shelf with aboriginal engravings of marine and land animals to view.

Description: Starting at Bundeena Wharf at the end of Brighton Street, follow the road up the hill and left onto Loftus Street. Continue along Loftus Street to the footpath at the intersection with Neil Street. Continue straight along the footpath down between the residential area and onto Jibbon Beach.

Once on Jibbon Beach, follow the track past the Royal National Park sign to the signposted Jibbon Loop Track near the end of Jibbon Beach. The loop is 3.2 km around.

Jibbon Loop is signposted and leads walkers along the coastline and on to one of the highlights of the walk, the aboriginal engravings site. There is an elevated platform from which you can view the engravings, including that of a whale, which is quite large.

Continue along the loop, taking in Jibbon Point back onto Jibbon Beach and back to toward Bundeena, retracing your steps through the streets to the Bundeena Wharf.

Along the Way:

The coastal view off Port Hacking is spectacular, the waters in the area are a sublime blue and the beach is at its most glorious along this stretch.

Closest Suburb: Bundeena

Start Location: Bundeena Wharf, at the end of Brighton Street, Bundeena.

Latitude and longitude: 34.083591°S, 151.151665°E

Grade: 3

Trail Quality: Street walking, beach walking and trail. Some obstacles underfoot. Some rocks to walk over.

Distance: 5.1 km

Time: 2 hours

Amenities: Yes, at the wharf

Park Type: Royal National Park

The large rock shelf adorned with aboriginal engravings is the highlight of this walk. There are marine and land animals etched into the rock and a large engraving of a whale.

Karloo Pools

Within just 2.8 km of the start of this walk, you will find a blissful waterhole that's ripe for a swim. The walk in and out is not onerous and the anticipation of a swim will keep you company along the way. There are plenty of places to picnic at Karloo Pools if you want to make a day of it.

Description: Starting at Heathcote Railway Station, make your way along Wilson Parade in a south-east direction. You will pass the Emergency Services Centre and see the sign posted 'Karloo Track'. Follow the Karloo track east away from the road. The Karloo track will lead you behind the Emergency Services Centre and down to Heathcote Brook. After crossing Heathcote Brook, you come to the intersection with Heathcote Brook Bushtrack. Follow this track east and along the ridgeline before dropping down into the valley to the Karloo Pools. The last section of the trail as it drops down to Karloo pools is rough underfoot.

Along the Way:
Karloo Pools are a great place for a swim on a hot day. The views on the ridgeline as it passes above Heathcote Brook track are vast – with views across the valley below.

Closest Suburb: Heathcote

Start Location: Heathcote Railway Station, Wilson Parade, Heathcote.

Latitude and longitude: 34.088069°S, 151.008399°E

Grade: 3

Trail Quality: Can be rough underfoot, some obstacles. Easily followed.

Distance: 5.6 km

Time: 3 hours

Amenities: Yes, at the railway station at Heathcote

Park Type: Royal National Park

Home to a plethora of bats, reptiles, birds and amphibians, it's worth taking your time to see what you can spot in the bushland and waterways. Bird lovers will enjoy watching over 300 species of birds which make their home in the Royal National Park. Species include Crimson Rosellas, Yellow-Tailed Black Cockatoos, Sulphur Crested Cockatoos and Rainbow Lorikeets. There is also sufficiently impressive flora to support the bird life in the area.

Federation Cliff Walking Track

With postcard views of the Pacific Ocean, this walk takes in the magnificent sandstone cliffs that explorers first saw when they reached the Sydney coastline. The vast blue of the ocean seems to command your gaze and in the winter months whales can be seen migrating. This walk is bound to impress with endless reserves, coastal views, waves breaking on the cliffs below, a lighthouse, a military battery and whale-watching for those happy to walk the cooler months.

Description: Make your way to the northern end of Dudley Page Reserve, leave the reserve via the steps in the northeast corner and walk left, along the pathway to the intersection of Military Road and Lancaster Road. Cross to the eastern side of the road. Make your way right, along Lancaster Road, following it to Eastern Reserve. The Federation Cliff Walking Track travels along to the north from here, through the reserve and along boardwalk before coming to a set of steps up to the corner of Oceanview Street and Ray Street. Follow Ray Street to the end and enter Diamond Bay Reserve.

   Diamond Bay Reserve is beautiful and the views sublime, and you may spend some time here. Follow the trail down the stairs for a much closer look at the cliffs and waves crashing below. Back on to boardwalk, continue along until you come to what seems like a pocket of rainforest. Take the ramp to your left up to Chris Bang Crescent. Follow Chris Bang Crescent to the right as it runs parallel to the cliff tops and loops to the left, then straight as it becomes Marne Street and then Jensen Avenue. This road section is approximately 550 metres.

   Make your way off the end of Jensen Avenue into Clarke Reserve where you pick up the trail again at the northern end of the reserve

Closest Suburb: Dover Heights

Start Location: Dudley Page Reserve, corner of Lancaster Road and Military Road, Dover Heights.

Latitude and longitude: 33.868447°S, 151.281620°E

Grade: 3

Trail Quality: Mostly sealed paths and grass, some roads, quite a few steps

Distance: 7.8 km

Time: 3 hours 30 minutes

Amenities: Yes

Park Type: Urban

Watsons Bay

The Gap

Don Ritchie
Grove

Macquarie Lighthouse

Vaucluse

Diamond Reserve

Old South Head Road

Eastern Reserve

Dover
Heights

Military Road

N

500 m

Raleigh Reserve

and where Macquarie Lighthouse is visible. After Macquarie Lighthouse, continue along the pathway through Lighthouse Reserve, past South Head Signal Station, Signal Hill Battery and Signal Hill Reserve. The section from here to Don Ritchie Grove has some amazing ocean views. Don Ritchie Grove is worth taking some time to soak in before continuing along the pathway to The Gap.

At the Gap, the Gap Bluff Walking Track leads to several viewing platforms where both whale watching and gazing out to sea is popular. There are some steps to the platforms, however they are worthwhile before making your return trip. Retrace your steps to return to the finish.

Along the Way:

Don Ritchie Grove is named in honour of a gentleman who resided next to The Gap. Over a period of 50 years it is thought he saved up to 400 lives of people who had made their way to the Gap to end their lives. Mr Ritchie had a simple recipe for people who were in a mentally vulnerable state. With a smile and a chat, he often invited these folks into his home to

talk. Mr Ritchie and his wife were recognised for their generosity of heart and compassion by both the Woollahra Council and the National Australia Day Council.

The cliffs at Raleigh Reserve span some 80 metres down to the ocean.

Signal Hill Battery was one in a set of three defence fortifications along the coastline of Sydney. The battery armaments, which were removed after World War II, were intended to be able to defend Sydney against bombardment from any enemy approaching from the coast. The battery has is more than it appears from the park, there is an underground complex which runs underneath Old South Head Road and, although long since closed to the public, it contains a mess room, corridors, a bevy of utility rooms and an elevator shaft.

If you would like to make a longer day of it, continue beyond the end of the walk to Watsons Bay where you will get some divine views of Sydney Harbour and enjoy a cool drink at the pub or one of many cafes. This would extend your walk by 2 km, or about 30 minutes, each way.

Iron Cove – The Bay Walk

A sealed walk around the picturesque Iron Cove Bay, which is fed from Parramatta River, this is a family-friendly walk with plenty to keep you intrigued along the way. The walk passes through seven suburbs, making it a local walk for thousands of people every day enjoying a day out. There are many parks and reserves along the way as well as cafes and benches on the foreshore. Rodd Park, located at Rodd Point is a great location to picnic midway through the walk.

Description: Starting at King George Park, make your way down to the waterfront, then turn left, following the path and keeping the water on your right. Continue along until the pathway spills onto Waterfront Drive, passing by Callan Park. After Callan Park the pathway restarts. Rodd Island can be seen across the bay and the walk continues past the Leichardt sports precinct, and through Hippo Park. There are public water facilities and amenities in Hippo Park. As you leave Hippo Park, make your way along the pathway parallel to Maliyawul Street and passing the Le Montage function centre. As the Lilyfield Road bridge comes into view, veer left and take the ramp up onto the bridge. Turn right, cross over Hawthorne Canal and continue with the water on your right.

The pathway parallels the City West Link along the foreshore, and continues past the Haberfield Rowers Club to the junction with Timbrell Drive. Take the right turn just prior Timbrell Drive and over Iron Cove Creek pedestrian bridge. Follow the pathway parallel with Timbrell Drive and as the mangroves thicken on your right, the pathway makes its way past Rodd Point and Rodd Park. Amenities are available at Rodd Point. The pathway hugs the foreshore and various inlets and

Closest Suburb: Close to the Sydney CBD

Start Location: King George Park, Manning Street, Rozelle.

Latitude and longitude: 33.862754°S, 151.164013°E

Grade: 2

Trail Quality: Smooth formed pathway, mostly flat. Easily followed.

Distance: 7 km

Time: 2 hours

Amenities: Yes, at King George Park and several other parks along the walk.

Park Type: Urban

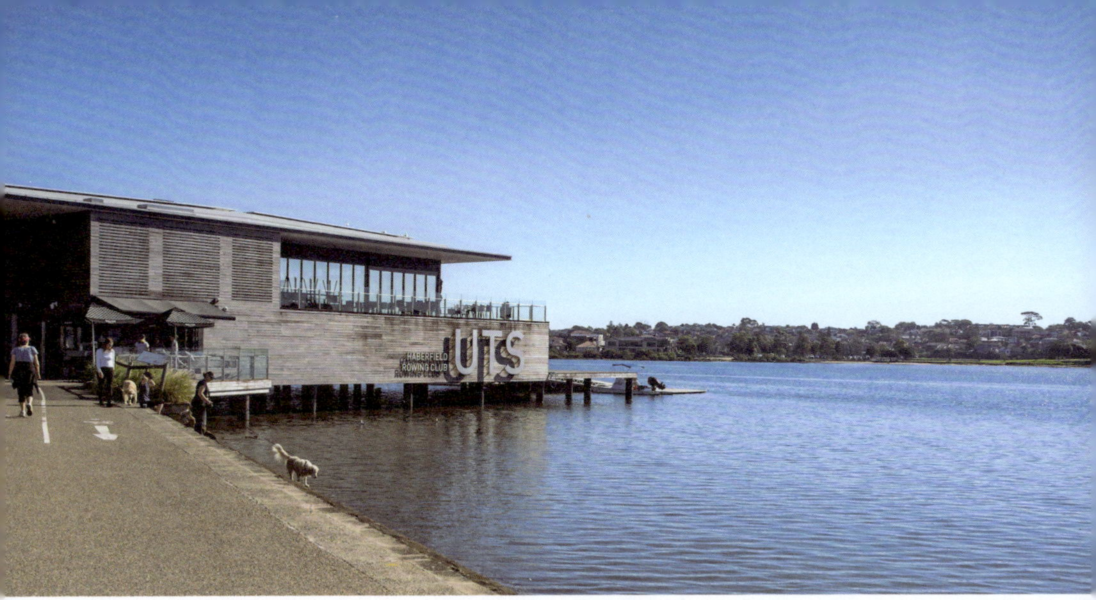
UTS
HABERFIELD
ROWING CLUB

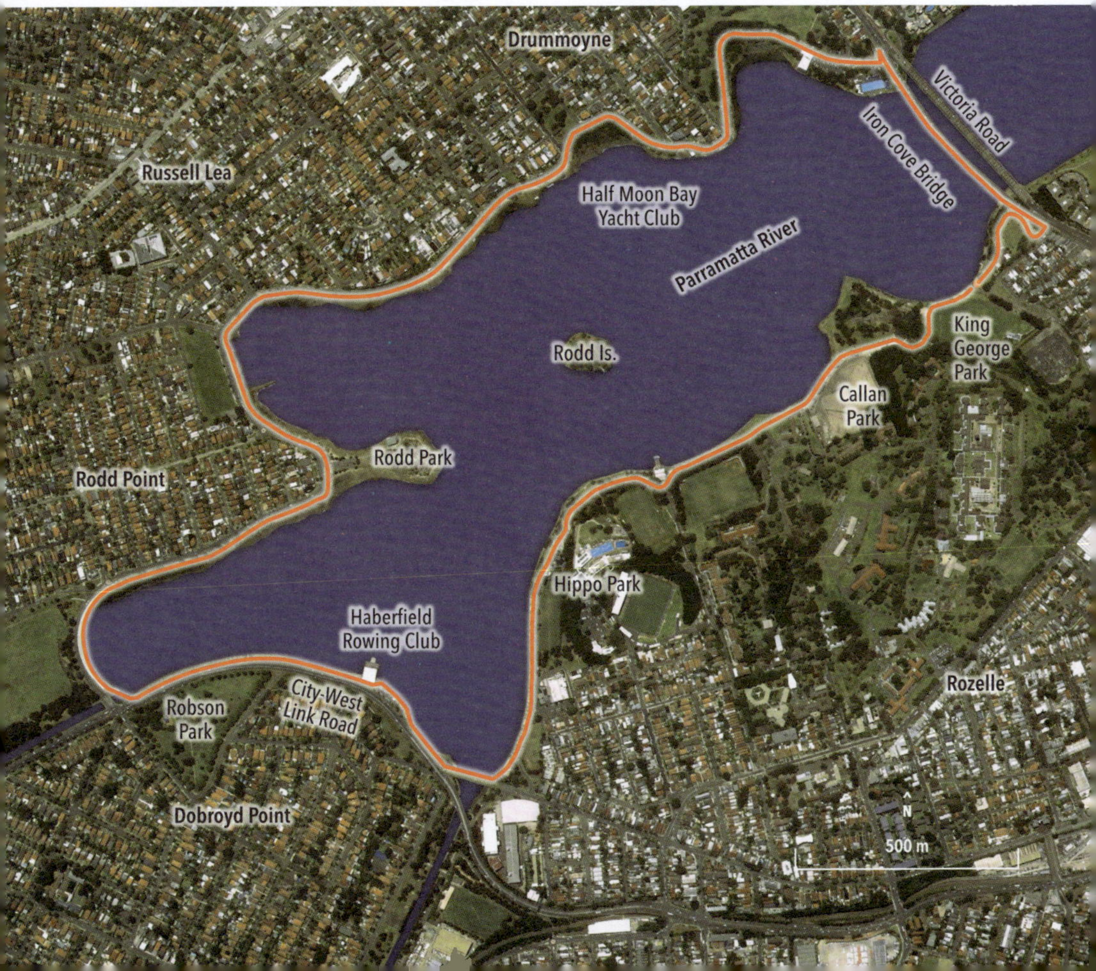
Drummoyne
Victoria Road
Iron Cove Bridge
Russell Lea
Half Moon Bay
Yacht Club
Parramatta River
King
George
Park
Rodd Is.
Callan
Park
Rodd Park
Rodd Point
Hippo Park
Haberfield
Rowing Club
Rozelle
Robson
Park
City-West
Link Road
Dobroyd Point
N
500 m

continues past the Half Moon Bay Yacht Club, Thompson Street Jetty and eventually onto Iron Cove Bridge. Turn right onto the bridge making your way from Drummoyne to Rozelle. Descend the bridge to your right, passing King Georges pontoon and into King Georges park for the finish.

Along the Way:

The Bay run passes through Rozelle, Lilyfield, Haberfield, Five Dock, Rodd Point, Russell Lea and Drummoyne.

Callan Park is a 61-hectare heritage listed property incorporating sandstone buildings and houses. The facility from inception has had a spectrum of names including, Callan Park Hospital for the Insane, Callan Park Mental Hospital, Callan Park Hospital and, most recently, Rozelle

Hospital. The historical site is now restricted to community, tertiary and health pursuits.

The habitats and ecosystem of the mangroves and mudflats that hug the shoreline of Timbrell Drive are detailed in information boards along this section of pathway.

Rodd Point and Rodd Park. Names after the Rodd Family who resided and contributed to the area from 1809, The Rodd family mausoleum was refurbished into a memorial with the bodies being moved to Rookwood Cemetery in 1903. Further to Rodd Island, Rodd Point and Rodd Park, streets around the suburb of Rodd Point are named after patriarch Brent Clements Rodd's family and their British heritage. His children's names: Janet, Lenore, Trevanion, Undine, Brisbane, Burnell, Brent and Clements all feature locally on street signs.

Rodd Island was previously known as Rabbit Island, Rhode Island, Snake Island and Jack Island. While each name has its own history, the Rabbit Island moniker is thought to have come into vogue in 1887 when, Sir Henry Parkes offered a £25,000 reward (equivalent to $10 million in today's money!) for anyone who could solve the plague-like proportions of Rabbits that were destroying the countryside. Louis Pasteur, who was himself working on a similar dilemma in France, sent his nephew, Doctor Adrien Loir to conduct the experiments in the facilities that were built on the island. By 1890, the experiments had yielded little hope of solving the rabbit problem and they started to produce livestock vaccines instead.

The first Iron Cove Bridge was opened in 1882 and linked Sydney to the west. In 1955, the current steel truss bridge, now heritage listed, replaced the old bridge and in in 2011 an additional bridge was constructed to carry the heavy flow of traffic, linking the suburbs of Rozelle and Drummoyne.

Lake Parramatta Reserve Walk

One of the most significant and beautiful bushland remnants in Western Sydney, completed in 1856, Lake Parramatta was the first large dam built in Australia and was a crucial part of the Parramatta City water supply until 1909. Today Lake Parramatta Reserve offers 4 short walk options, the Heritage Path, Arrunga Bardo, Reservoir Track and Upper Lake Track which when combined circumnavigate the lake creating the Lake Circuit Track.

A culturally significant site, once the home of the Burramatagal clan, remnants of aboriginal times including middens, hand stencils and remnant shelters can be seen.

The diversity of the flora and fauna is apparent as you walk around the pathways and the reserve has been proclaimed a Wildlife Refuge to protect what lies within.

Closest Suburb: North Parramatta

Start Location: The main entrance is via Lackey St North Parramatta, off Bourke St. The entrance is called Illawong Drive, but Google Maps doesn't recognise that.

The entry gates open between 6:30am and 5:30pm (7:30pm during daylight savings).

Latitude and longitude:
33.791091°S, 151.007486°E

Grade: 3

Trail Quality: sealed pathways, trail, some obstacles underfoot.

Distance: 4.2 km

Time: 2 hours

Amenities: Yes

Park Type: Lake Parramatta Reserve

Description: The Lake Circuit Track is made up of 4 walks, The Heritage Path, the Reservoir Track, The Upper Lake Track and the Arrunga Bardo Track. Each track leads onto the next and there is ample signposting along the way. The café at the Visitors Hub keeps copies of the Lake Parramatta Reserve Map for visitors.

Along the Way:

There are signboards at the visitor's hub detailing the history of the area and signs indicate flora species of interest.

The dam was built on the Hunts Creek in 1856 and the dam walls were fashioned from large sandstone blocks which were quarried onsite. In 1898, an extra 3.3 metres of height was added to the dam wall.

Walk 1: The Heritage Path

Grade: 1   **Distance:** 300 m

Starting at the visitor hub, follow the sealed pathway to the Dam Wall Lookout. From the Dam lookout, follow the signs to Reservoir Track.

Walk 2: Reservoir Track

Grade: 3   **Distance:** 600 m

Make your way along the Reservoir Track to the Reservoir lookout and then follow the signs onto the Upper Lake Track.

Walk 3: The Upper Lake Track

Grade: 3   **Distance:** 2.1 km

The Upper Lake Track circles the furthest section of the lake and connects the Reservoir Track with the Arrunga Bardo Walk at the Arrunga Bardo Lookout.

Walk 4: Arrunga Bardo Walk

Grade: 2   **Distance:** 900 m

Follow the signposted Arrunga Bardo Walk to the visitors hub.

North Rocks Road

The Upper Lake Track

The Upper Lake Track

Reservoir Track

The Heritage Path

Lake Parramatta

Arrunga Bardo Walk

James Ruse Drive

N

100 m

The Heritage Trail

The Heritage Trail takes in the valleys, trails and pathways through what was once thriving farmland in the Baulkham Hills area. Throughout the walk there are interesting interpretive signs detailing some of the stories of early settlers to the area. Colonial settlers sought to make a living from the land before the end of the 18th century. Although it has a history steeped in farming, the area is also known for the endangered vegetation community which protects one of the last Sydney Turpentine Ironbark forests.

Closest Suburb: Baulkham Hills

Start Location: Torry Burn Reserve. Start at the corner of Vanessa Avenue and Astrid Avenue, Baulkham Hills.

Latitude and longitude: 33.752609°S, 150.983653°E

Grade: 1

Trail Quality: Paved pathways. Some street crossings – use the pedestrian safety points to cross roads. The route is marked with the Heritage Trail logo.

Distance: 6.8 km

Time: 2 hours 30 minutes

Amenities: Toilets and picnic facilities are available at Crestwood Reserve approximately halfway through the walk.

Park Type: Baulkham Hills Shire Council

Description: From the Torry Burn Reserve, walk to the bridge and cross over it, once across, turn right and make your way through the Blackbutt woodland. Here you will see the first of the interpretive signs detailing the story of John Smith who named his property 'Torry Burn' after his hometown in Scotland. Walk on to Jasper Road and cross at the pedestrian refuge, continuing along the path into the endangered vegetation community that is the Sydney Turpentine Ironbark Forest.

From the Sydney Turpentine Ironbark Forest and making your way through Sophia Doyle Reserve, take the left option at the fork in the track and continue downhill to Toongabbie Creek. Sophia Doyle was a first settler on this land and the interpretive sign tells her story. As you continue, turn right at the T-junction and shortly after descending into the valley amongst the Blackbutts.

As you reach Seven Hills Road, the story of William Joyce, a land grant

recipient, is detailed on the next interpretive sign. 150 metres further on take the path to the right. On the left side of Seven Hills Road is Matthew Pearce Public School, Matthew Pearce was one of the largest landowners in Baulkham Hills. The path continues through part of Mr Pearce's land to the crossing on Merindah Road and then on to Peel Road and the Crestwood Reserve. Take the path to the left and the amenities and picnic areas become apparent.

From Crestwood Reserve, cross over the bridge to the interpretive sign detailing Major Joseph Foveaux who, in 1799, was granted the land as part of his Stock Farm. Cross back over the bridge and continue on the path on the right side of the creek, through Crestwood Reserve past the outdoor gym equipment and along the footpath on Peel Road to Kalimna Drive.

Cross over Peel Road and continue walking to Benwerrin Avenue, turn right along Benwerrin Avenue and make your way to Merindah Road. Turn right, cross the road at the intersection with Glanmire Road, travelling along Glanmire Road towards Turon Avenue Reserve. Prior to the bend, cross the road into Turon Reserve south of Lisgar Avenue and follow the track. At the next track junction in the reserve turn left and walk to Turon Avenue, cross and turn left into Kent Street. Walk along Kent Street, turn left into Palace

Road and at St James Avenue turn right and walk to Geraldine Avenue. Turn right into Geraldine Avenue and left into Astrid Avenue to finish.

Along the Way:

Interpretive signs along the way detail the stories of the early settlers in the area. Many of the parks and reserves are also named after these local identities.

Classified as an endangered vegetation community, the Sydney Turpentine Ironbark Forest (STIF) grows on fertile soil in the area and was cut down as settlers encroached to make way for farmland. Currently it is estimated that only 0.5% of STIF remains in Sydney.

Binyang Matta Trail

Dubbed as Sydney's biggest backyard, the Western Sydney Parklands is located within the Blacktown, Liverpool and Fairfield council areas and encompassing over 5000 hectares of bushland with over 60 km of pathways and trails to explore. The Bintang Matta Track, meaning 'place of birds' in the Dharug language, is a popular trail for families and the area has an abundance of open spaces to relax and enjoy a picnic or barbeque after exploring the trails.

Description: Starting at the Richmond Road carpark, the 6.7 km loop winds its way along sealed paths through grasslands, wetlands and forested sections. The pathway is easily followed and signposted with meter-high signs at the intersections. A map is also available from the Western Sydney Parklands website. As you make your way around the loop, you will cross Eastern Creek several times and observe some of the many bird species the area boasts. Keep a look out for Swift Parrots and Azure Kingfishers as you explore the parklands.

Closest Suburb: Dean Park

Start Location: Carpark on the north side of Richmond Road, Dean Park, between the Quakers Hill Parkway and Symonds Rd.

Latitude and longitude: 33.741279°S, 150.867018°E

Grade: 1

Trail Quality: Sealed path and some connecting street walking.

Distance: 6.7 km

Time: 2 hours

Amenities: Closest amenities are at Joe McAleer Park. There are toilets and a café at Nurragingy Reserve, Eastern Creek, and a water bubbler at Richmond Road car park.

Park Type: Western Sydney Parklands

Dogs on leashes are welcome to walk with you through the parklands.

Along the Way:

Birdlife is abundant in the parklands and if you wish to get a close-up view, take some binoculars and leave some extra time in your schedule.

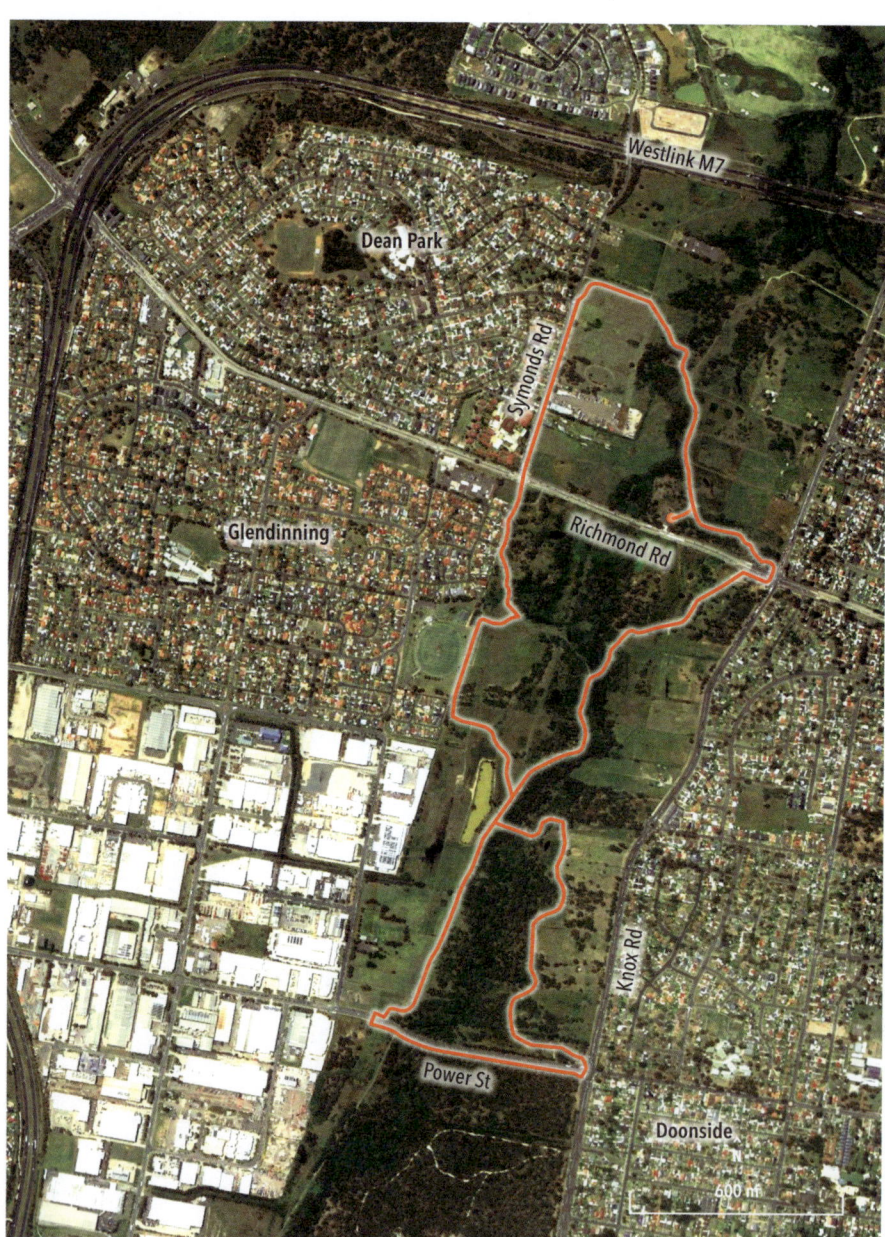

Fairylands Loop Track

The Fairyland Walk is a lovely green pocket of trail that partly uses a small section of the much longer Great North Walk (250 km). Located just 20 minutes from the Sydney CBD, the track is challenging and rewarding with views of the Lane Cove River, some sublime picnic areas to stop and rest and some interesting suburban walking.

Description: From the intersection of River Avenue, near Delhi Road, the Fairylands Loop track starts by following the signposted 'Great North Walk (GNW) – Sydney Cove' Trail.

Closest Suburb: Chatswood

Start Location: Fullers Bridge carpark at the intersection of River Avenue and Delhi Road at Chatswood West.

Latitude and longitude: 33.792990°S, 151.156226°E

Grade: 4

Trail Quality: Occasionally rough trail, uneven steps of stone and timber, boardwalk, sealed path and some grassy paddock walking.

Distance: 5.3 km

Time: 2 hours 30 minutes

Amenities: At the start and finish there are amenities on the north side of Delhi Road.

Park Type: Lane Cove National Park

Leading up steep rock steps that have been cut into the hillside, the track winds uphill passing several GNW arrow posts along the way. Continue to climb the steps and trail through some large boulders and onto a large rock platform where the trail veers left and levels out. Approximately 170m onwards you will come to a locked gate at the end of Quebec Road.

Follow Quebec Road past the junction with Fairylands Avenue and continue to follow Quebec Rd as it leads left and downhill. Near the bottom of the hill and prior to Quebec Road turning left again, there is another GNW arrow post indicating the direction to follow. Follow the track until you see the sign 'Lane Cove National Park – Fairyland Track'. Continue over the boardwalk and to the rock platform and your first grand views of the Land Cove River are on your left. Caution should be taken here as the rock platform is unfenced and there is a significant drop off.

From this viewing point, the track gives some respite with a welcomed flat trail before it starts to descend timber steps to the boardwalk below and the Fairylands Pleasure Grounds. There is an information board detailing

the Fairylands Pleasure Grounds and a short walk further on leads to a short track to the left with a well-used seat beside the Lane Cove River.

From the seat, continue straight and follow the GNW arrow posts, keeping a view of the Lane Cove River on your left through the trees until you reach more boardwalk. Following the boardwalk, you reach the 'Site of Fairyland Pleasure Grounds' sign. Follow the dirt and timber steps upwards and out of the old pleasure grounds, cornering left and climbing to the top of the hill where the track then leads downhill to the signposted intersection and another GNW arrow post. The trail continues through undulating terrain, crossing several bridges before reaching steps leading to a wide shared footpath beside Epping Road. Follow the GNW arrow markers across the bridge and down the steps onto the trail. Continue on the trail on the other side of the bridge. Make your way under the bridge and continuing along the river bank until you reach a carpark where you veer right and walk up the steps winding around the hill past the oval and above the spectators stand. Continue across the grassed area to Mowbray Park. Keeping the valley of the river on your left, continue to walk uphill away from the athletics oval through the bushland and to a signposted intersection. From the intersection the track passes a large boulder on the left and continues to another signposted intersection. Veer right here and follow the Lane Cove River, keeping the river on your left until you reach a boardwalk and another signposted intersection. The track follows the arrow signs for the 'River Track'. You will come to several intersections and suspended boardwalks that cross mangroves, continue to follow the River Track arrow signs, keeping the river on your left and eventually emerging behind the 8th hole at Chatswood Golf Course.

Continue to the left of the 8th fairway, hugging the treeline with the river on your left and you will come to another signposted intersection. Continue straight, again following the Lane Cove River under the shade of the river bank trees and to the intersection of Delhi Road and Lady Game Drive. Take a sharp left, downhill and under Fullers Bridge where you meet the footpath next to Lady Game Drive. Turn right and come to the intersection of Delhi Road where you then cross Fullers Bridge and down the steps to your right (before the bus stop).

Follow the pathway under Fullers Bridge to the end of the minor road and past the Riverside Café Bar and Grill. Turn right in front of the Café and along the road to the T-intersection with River Avenue and where you started your walk.

Along the Way:

The Fairyland Pleasure Grounds – also informally known as 'The Rest' was a 17-acre plot of land purchased by Robert Swan in 1896. In its early days, part of the land was developed into market gardens however the market gardens were gone by the early 1900s and the area became a popular picnic and recreation area for immigrants. Today the area, with nature reclaiming some of the cleared areas, continues to provide respite from the city bustle, with plenty of opportunities to relax by the river.

The Fairyland Circuit provides the opportunity for plentiful birdlife experiences including lorikeets and Kookaburras. Along the river's edge you are likely to encounter Eastern Water Dragons enjoying a sunny aspect.

Wildflower Gardens – The Mueller Track

In what feels like Sydney's best kept secret, the Ku-ring-gai Wildflower Gardens span 123 hectares of pristine bushland with plenty of trails for walking, appreciating the much and varied flora and the intriguing fauna that it supports.

The most rugged and remote of the walks within the Ku-ring-gai Wildflower Gardens, the Mueller Track follows the waters of the Ku-ring-gai creek through stands of tall red gums before it falls gently down the spectacular Phantom Falls and into Tree Fern Gully Creek. Walkers are treated to Whipbird Gully, a spot to stop and rest and refresh. There are smaller sets of waterfalls along the way. Known for its magnificent flora, the wildflower gardens will delight those looking for a rich flora experience.

Description: Before starting out, it is worth ducking into the Visitors Centre – across from Dampier's Clearing Picnic Area – to get a map of the area. The back of the map details some good information about the Wildflower Gardens including picnic areas.

Starting at the Visitors Centre, the walk starts by heading briefly down

Closest Suburb: St Ives 2075

Start Location: Parking is at the Visitors Centre off Richmond Ave, 420 Mona Vale Rd, St Ives, 2075.

Latitude and longitude: 33.707411°S, 151.174906°E

Grade: 4

Trail Quality: Narrow and hilly trail in places, obstacles underfoot. Can be muddy in wet conditions.

Distance: 3 km

Time: 2 hours

Amenities: Yes

Park Type: Ku-ring-gai Wildflower Garden

the sealed Solander Track before turning left into the signposted Mueller Track, which meanders through open forest. Predominantly a flora walk, the first part of the walk shows off the Grass Trees (*Xanthorrhoea* sp.), while the cooler months give life to the bright flowers of the Old Man Banksia (*Banksia Serrata*) and Silver Banksia (*Banksia marginata*). If visiting in Spring expect a colour bomb of red from Red Spider Grevillea (*Grevillea speciosa*) and Mountain Devils (*Lambertia Formosa*). Further along and upon reaching some deep sandy soils the Red Bloodwood and Scribby Gums become plentiful.

The Mueller Track continues through rocky outcrops and makes its way downhill and past the turnoff to the Fitzgerald track on your right. The track then passes through a gap in two large sandstone rocks and descends toward Ku-ring-gai Creek. Once at the creek, the canopy species changes as the more fertile and moist soils dominate. The track walks alongside the creek and the floral aroma can be strong and fresh in the springtime. Sweet Pittosporum (*Pittosporum undulatum*) is plentiful in this section of the walk encouraging Currawong and other birds with its bright orange berries.

As you approach Phantom Falls, there is a large outcrop overlooking the falls which is a great place for viewing taking in the views. Bird calls

are plentiful in the area and combined with the sound of the tumbling waters make for a peaceful auditory experience. From the outcrop, the track descends through a She-oak (*Allocasuarina*) forest towards Whipbird Gully. The She-oak seeds provide a high-quality food source for the endangered Black Glossy Cockatoo so it is worth keeping your sights skyward as you make your way into Whipbird Gully.

Continuing past Whipbird Gully, the track is now running alongside Tree Fern Gully Creek and starts to ascend. As you come to the large hanging rock and onwards across Billy's Bridge, a natural rock arch, you will notice an abundance of species of ferns in this area. The track winds back up towards Lamberts Clearing and the open forest that was seen during the first part of the walk, then back to the Visitor Centre.

Along the Way:

As you encounter banksia, be on the lookout for signs of the Eastern Pygmy Possum and Wattle birds which feed on the nectar of the flowers.

Take a close look at the Scribbly markings that give the Scribbly Gum its name. These marks are the results of moth larva activity as they burrow under the bark leaving 'scribbly' trails.

As you pass through the gap in the sandstone rocks, inspect some of the small crevices and caves in the rocks, they provide protected habitat for small marsupial mice species such as the Brown Antechinus.

Birrawanna Walking Track

With the possibility of an Emu sighting, this is a challenging walking track finishing at beautiful Bobbin Head, a prime location for a picnic. Along the way, there are some impressive flora including the vibrant waratahs. Scribby gums are sure to activate your imagination with their curious markings and the views over Cowan Water and Cockle Creek are captivating.

Description: At the start/finish of the Birrawanna Walk, the Kalkari Discovery Centre offers an immersive, interactive experience with the flora, fauna and aboriginal history of the Ku-ring-gai Chase National Park. Signposted, this walk is predominantly downhill to Bobbin Head. You will pass by the emu enclosure as you wind your way toward beautiful views over Cowan Water. The last part of the walk can be challenging as the footing is uneven.

After exploring the waterside of Bobbin Head, retrace your steps back to the Kalkari Discovery Centre along the route you came.

Closest Town: Mt Colah

Start Location: Kalkari Discovery Centre, 402 Ku-ring-gai Chase Road, Mt Colah 2079.

Latitude and longitude: 33.665538°S, 151.148997°E

Grade: 3

Trail Quality: Formed track, some obstacles, many steps, steep in places, rough underfoot in places.

Distance: 4 km

Time: 2 hours

Amenities: Yes, at the start

Park Type: Ku-ring-gai Chase National Park.

Along the Way:

The Kalkari Discovery Centre offers an inspirational and immersive experience in the flora, fauna and aboriginal history of the Ku-ring-gai Chase National Park.

The Birrawanna Walk skirts the Emu enclosure which, if you spot an Emu, could be an excellent photo opportunity.

Bobbin Head

Bobbin Head
Information Centre

Ku-Ring-Gai
Chase Rd

Apple Tree Creek

Cockle Creek

Cowan
Water

Bobbin Head Rd

N

300 m

Kalkari Discovery
Centre

Aboriginal Heritage Walk

A challenging walk and a remarkable cultural experience. Ku-ring-gai Chase National Park is home to one of the largest collections of Aboriginal cultural sites in Australia. These sites evidence the tribal life and culture that forever changed after European settlement.

The Aboriginal Heritage Walk combines the West Head and Resolute Walking Tracks to showcase the rock engravings and art of the traditional owners of the Ku-ring-gai Chase National Park area. The area has a bounty of flora and fauna to admire and the West Head Lookout, once seen will become a great mental memento of the walk.

Description: Clearly signposted, this track is easy to follow and allows you to spend time appreciating the many features as you come across them. From the carpark, walk through the Resolute Picnic Area and follow the sign marked 'Red Hands Track 50m'. Descend the stairs and continue straight.

The first site of interest, Red Hands Cave, features ancient prints on the sandstone walls, painted with traditional technique in ochre.

Closest Suburb: Terrey Hills

Start Location: Resolute Picnic Area, West Head Road, West Head precinct of the Ku-ring-gai Chase National Park.

Latitude and longitude: 33.578222°S, 151.300375°E

Grade: 4

Trail Quality: Rough track, many obstacles, many steps, very steep in places. Clearly signposted.

Distance: 4.4 km

Time: 3 hours

Amenities: Yes, at Resolute Picnic Area

Park Type: Ku-ring-gai Chase National Park

From Red Hands Cave, continue straight, and after the steps, the track directs you left where you continue to climb to the junction with the service trail. This is signposted. Turn left here and follow the trail downhill to where it meets the information board and the engravings at West Head. Made by the Guringai people, the engravings show both man and sea creatures.

After the engravings the trail follows the service road up the hill from the information board, ignoring the turn off to Red Hands Cave and continuing straight onwards to the picnic ground.

Along the Way:

There are interpretive signs along the track which give valuable information about each point of interest.

The Red Hands Cave is a small rock overhang with traditional aboriginal paintings on the walls. These paintings are thought to be approximately 2000 years old. The Hands paintings were made using one of two traditional methods of painting. The first, an outspread hand is held over the 'canvas' (rock) and the clay mixture, an ochre colour is blown from the mouth to create negative image of the hand. The second method involved covering the hand with clay and pressing against the rock to create a positive image.

You will notice that some aboriginal hand paintings depict the wrist and forearm in addition to the handprint, and at some sites the hands sit at different heights. Status was indicated by the position of the hands on the wall, and whether the wrist and forearm were included. The higher positioned hands with wrist and forearm were thought to belong to Aboriginal Elders and reflected their status.

West Head provides some magnificent views and is the site of the engravings of which there are two eels, a man and a shark or whale.

Bairne Walking Track to Towlers Bay Lookout

One of the more leisurely walks in Ku-ring-gai Chase National Park, the Bairne Walking Track takes you out to Towlers Bay Lookout where there are sublime views over the waters of Towlers Bay and Pittwater. You are bound to see more wildlife than humans on this walk, including wallabies, goannas and various lizards sunning themselves on the rock shelves. The rock shelf of Towlers Bay Lookout provides a great spot for a picnic or simply to spend some time watching the boats below glide by.

Description: From West Head Road, the Bairne Walking Track is signposted. Walk along the formed trail for 2.5 km until you reach a fork in the track. Turn right and follow the signed walk 1.1 km to Towlers Bay Lookout. Along the way there are two short downhills, and the rest of the walk is on relatively flat ground. This walk is well signposted.

Returning, leave Towlers Bay Lookout and return to the junction where you turn left, following Bairne Walking Track back to the carpark.

Along the Way:

Flora: Banksia, Boronia and Grevillea highlight the typical coastal Australian bushland on this walk. During August and September the wildflowers are at their finest and line the trail all the way to Towlers Bay Lookout. Be sure to look for the magnificent grove of Waratah in the first section of the walk.

Fauna: A bird watchers paradise the variegated fairy wren and yellow faced honeyeaters are plentiful. Wallabies, although shy will sit in the

Closest Suburb: Terrey Hills

Start Location: Intersection of the Bairne Walking Track and West Head Road, Ku-ring-Gai Chase, Ku-ring-gai Chase National Park. The track is marked by a locked gate and a 'Bairne Track' sign.

Latitude and longitude: 33.607781°S, 151.269833°E

Grade: 3

Trail Quality: Formed track, short steep inclines, occasional steps. Well signposted.

Distance: 7.2 km

Time: 2 hours 30 minutes

Amenities: No

Park Type: Ku-ring-gai Chase National Park

heathland and spectate, while goannas will begrudgingly move from their sun drenched rocks to allow you passage.

Central Coast and Hunter Valley

Patonga to Pearl Beach Walking Track

Although a small part of the 250 kilometre iconic Great North Walk, part of the journey between Patonga and Pearl Beach contributes to the celebration of the 1988 bicentenary. While the Great North Walk links Sydney with Newcastle, this walk links Patonga Beach with Pearl Beach and offers spectacular views and scenery. Walking beach to beach – the walk gives a sense of both challenge and achievement.

Description: From the parking at the Patonga Wharf carpark, you can pick up the Great North Walk direction posts and follow them along the footpaths to the Eastern end of Patonga Beach where Brisbane Water National Park starts and the track starts.

Alternatively, you can walk down the beach on the sand, past the Warrah Reserve Boat Ramp to what

Closest Town: Patonga 2256

Start Location: Patonga Wharf, Patonga Drive, Patonga.

Latitude and longitude: 33.550413°S, 151.274584°E

Grade: 5

Trail Quality: Formed track, very steep and difficult in some areas, some obstacles. Limited signposts.

Distance: 6 km

Time: 3 hours

Amenities: Yes

Park Type: Brisbane Water National Park

is known as Dark Corner, the eastern end of Patonga Beach and where the track starts.

From the eastern end of Patonga Beach, follow the signs marked 'Warrah Trig', making your way up the steps, winding upwards and following the ridgeline and the Great North Walk direction poles. After passing a stand of Sydney Red Gums, the track comes to a large rock platform and the beautiful views over Broken Bay.

After taking in the views of Broken Bay and having a breather from the previous climb, veer left and continue along the Great North Walk, again uphill. With the ocean to your right, the surrounding bushland occasionally reveals glimpses of the bright blue waters below. As you come to a clear intersection meeting the Pearl Beach Patonga fire trail, veer to the right and continue to follow the Great North Walk directional signs for approximately

350 metres. (There are two tracks to the right within 100 metres of each other, the first is marked with large boulders, ignore this track). The second is at an intersection marked with a Patonga directional sign. The track to your right is the track to Warrah lookout, a fenced lookout worth the 150 metre deviation.

After leaving Warrah lookout, retrace your steps and turn right back onto the Pearl Beach/Patonga Fire Trail that trends downhill, soon revealing views over Pearl Beach. Continue along the trail, as it passes between two large rocks and just left under some sandstone caves in the cliff face. These are the Pearl Caves.

From the Pearl Caves, continue downhill along the track past the locked gate and sign indicating 'Pearl Beach/Patonga Fire Trail'. Continue downhill and right onto Crystal Ave, turn left onto Diamond Road and right onto Amethyst Ave to the forefront of Pearl Beach.

Return the way you came, there is signage along the way which indicates the way to Patonga Beach.

Along the Way:

Broken Bay viewing point – This unnamed lookout east of Patonga is shaded by Sydney Red Gums and has great views across the Hawkesbury River, Cowan Creek to West Head, and past Lion Island to Barrenjoey Head.

Warrah Lookout – A more formal lookout, fenced for safety, follow the sandstone pathway for a short distance to magnificent panoramic views from the southern boundary of the Brisbane Water National Park through to Patonga. Views take in Barrenjoey Headland, West Head and Juno Point.

Pearl Caves – The Pearl Beach / Patonga fire trail is home to the 'Pearl Caves'. These caves are large overhangs and not maintained or fenced. Exploration reveals some stalactites and stalagmites in the back of one of the caves.

Pearl Beach – with a population of just over 500 people, is a blissful oasis. The beach is 1.2 km long and has an ocean pool at the southern end. There is a Café on Pearl Parade if you are looking for a lunch before returning to Patonga.

Mount Bouddi, Bouddi Coastal Track, Maitland Bay Circuit

The views from Bouddi Lookout command deep contemplation as the ocean air meets the background of the Bouddi Grand Deep Rainforest. In the winter months, there is a good chance of spotting whales migrating. During low tide, it is likely you will spot the remnants of the wreckage of the SS *Maitland* as you descend onto Maitland Bay Beach. The Bouddi Coastal Track wanders across the serene beach of Maitland Bay and the Maitland Bay trail takes you up to the popular Maitland Bay Information Centre. Finish at the Mount Bouddi Picnic area and enjoy the barbeque facilities in a peaceful bush setting.

Closest Town: McMasters Beach

Start Location: Mount Bouddi Picnic Area, Mount Bouddi Road. Off The Scenic Road, Macmasters Beach.

Latitude and longitude: 33.5162980°S, 151.4033030°E

Grade: 4

Trail Quality: Rough underfoot, some steps, sand walking and steep inclines. Clearly signposted.

Distance: 6.2 km

Time: 3 hours

Amenities: Yes, at the start

Park Type: Bouddi National Park

Description: Dingeldei Picnic Area, commonly referred to as Mount Bouddi Picnic Area, is the start of this walk. Pass by the sandstone building and follow the sign to 'Little Beach'. The walk to the Bouddi Lookout includes a few sets of steps. Once at Bouddi Lookout, take in the vast views over Maitand Bay and Bouddi Point headland. Continue toward the coastline to join the Bouddi Coastal Track and the next leg of the walk.

At the junction with the Bouddi Coastal Track, turn right and begin the journey along the coastline, dropping down onto the beach for a walk across the Maitland Bay foreshore. During low tide you may spot the sparse remnants of the wrecked SS *Maitland* on the rocks near the headland at the eastern end of the beach. Continue along the beach and make your way onto the track just before the end of the beach. Following the signs at the junction to 'Maitland Bay Parking Area', this is where you depart from the Bouddi Coastal Track. The Maitland Bay track crosses a small bridge and climbs up through the forest to a rock platform with commanding views back over the bay. There are steps along this section, and it is steep in parts. After 1 kilometre, you are at the Maitland Bay Information Centre.

From the Information Centre, follow the signs for 'Stroms Track' which loops around to the top of Mount Bouddi Road. Turn right and follow Mount Bouddi Road to the finish at Mount Bouddi Picnic area.

Along the Way:

Mount Bouddi Picnic Area houses Dingeldei Memorial Shelter which was built in 1962 to commemorate the contributions of A.W (Bill) Dingeldei who was a trustee of the park. Today the picnic area is a quiet reflective picnic area with picnic tables, barbeques facilities and amenities.

Bouddi Lookout offers stunning views across the heath covered headlands to the Pacific Ocean. This is the first look at the radiant blue waters before making your way down onto the Bouddi Coastal Track.

Maitland Beach spans across Maitland Bay and was named after the SS *Maitland*, a paddle steamer and passenger ship, which crashed onto the rocks in 1898. The survivors of the shipwreck included a young baby, Daisy Hammond, whose ashes were scattered at the site of the wreck when she passed away in 1988 at the age of 90. Over 20 people lost their lives in the wreck. Wreckage can be seen at the eastern end of the beach during low tide.

Formerly the Maitland Store, the Maitland Bay Information Centre is a hub for local tourism and is open on weekends and public holidays.

Piles Creek Loop

A challenging and intense walk with an abundance of diverse landmarks to keep you intrigued. Lookouts, creek crossings, sandstone overhangs and caves, a suspension bridge, deep gorge and waterfall. This walk has it all and that's before considering the flora and fauna of the area. The Girrakool Picnic Area also provides a great start/ finish with facilities for barbequing and picnicking.

Description: From the picturesque Girrakool Picnic ground, make your way to the lower picnic area by following the 'Great North Walk' sign. Turn right onto the 'Pile Creek Loop Track' as per the next sign. The first stop along the way is at the Broula Lookout. Access the lookout by turning left onto the Broula Lookout Track, leaving the main pathway for a short walk to the lookout.

Once there, a filtered view of Piles Creek Waterfall gives walkers a taste of what's to come on the walk through the Piles Creek area. Once finished at the lookout, return along the Broula Lookout track and turn left onto the

main pathway and continue straight following the Girrakool Loop sign down to the Illoura Lookout. Continue on from the lookout, again following the Girrakool Loop sign and with the green fence on your left. At the next intersection, veer left and follow the Piles Creek Loop signs down the rocky steps crossing the concrete footbridge over Leask Creek. The next stop along the way is the Bundilla Lookout, which is a slight diversion to the left. Returning to the main track, turn left and continue as the track

Closest Town: Kariong

Start Location: Girrakool Picnic Area, end of Girrakool Road, Somersby.

Latitude and longitude: 33.431288°S, 151.276727°E

Grade: 5

Trail Quality: Steep and difficult, many steps, obstacles under foot, slippery rocks, rough track, stepping-stones and a suspension bridge. Limited signage.

Distance: 4 km

Time: 3 hours

Amenities: Yes

Park Type: Brisbane Water National Park

makes its way down the hill. The next portion of trail makes its way along rock steps and giant rocks and tracks up and down until it comes to a large rock overhang.

The sandstone overhangs of various sizes in this area are unofficially known as the 'Western Piles Creek Caves'. It's a lovely cool place to sit and reflect. Continue on from the caves section and into the bush where the trails cross several foot bridges, passes caves and crosses over the creek making its way to the clearing at the Phil Houghton Suspension Bridge.

Crossing the bridge, follow the trail down the stairs and turn left, past the old bridge and start to climb uphill. This area is steep and rocky and at the next intersection, turn left and follow the 'Girrakool' sign as the track makes its way to Rat Gully. Continue along the trail in this section, past a fenced lookout and an imposing rocky monolith to another cave that sits to the left of the track.

From the cave, continue through the fissure in the rock and to the timber stairway. Before making your way onto the stairway, turn left and travel along to the lookout over Piles Creek and the Valleys below. Retracing your steps, this time take the timber stairway and continue until you reach the next intersection. Again, follow the Girrakool sign as the track now passes by more sandstone overhangs and creek crossings landing at the top of the Piles Creek Waterfall. Cross the stepping stones and follow the wooden steps enroute to Illoura Lookout. Follow the Girrakool Loop sign up the stone steps, and when you intersect with the Broula Lookout Track, continue along the Girrakool Loop. Carpark signs indicate the Girrakool Picnic area and finish of the walk is just ahead.

Along the Way:
The trails and lookouts in the local area are all titled from aboriginal words.

Girrakool – 'place of still waters'.
Broula – 'place of trickling water'
Illoura – 'a peaceful or pleasant place'
Bundilla – 'meeting of waters'

Tour de Rumbalara Reserve

Tour the trails of the Rumbalara Reserve and get back to nature just a few minutes from Gosford. This walk features diverse landscapes and vegetation, great viewing points and passes by three of the bronze sculptures that were commissioned to celebrate the bicentenary in 1987. It is suggested to pack a picnic and stop at the Yaruga Picnic Area for a rest and relax midway through this walk.

Description: After parking at the Environmental Education Centre, make your way to the track head at the back of the buildings. Follow the walking trail signs up the steps and continue along the track. Cross the bridge and climb up to the management track intersection. Turn right and walk uphill to the intersection with the Casuarina Track. Take the staircase following the picnic area arrow, continue along the sandstone pathway to the track information board at the next intersection. Turn right, following the management trail down towards the gate at the bottom of the hill.

Pass the Rumbalara Reserve signpost on your left and into the parking area, follow the management track left and downhill, away from John Whiteway Drive. With the fence on your right, continue and follow the sign directing to White Street through the serene forest. From the intersection, follow the

Closest Town: Gosford

Start Location: Rumbalara Environmental Education Centre, corner of Donnison Street and John Whiteway Drive, Gosford.

Latitude and longitude: 33.427675°S, 151.347612°E

Grade: 4

Trail Quality: Metal and Sandstone steps, can be rough underfoot, mix of formed track and management track. Clearly Signposted.

Distance: 6.1 km

Time: 3 hours

Amenities: Yes, at the start

Park Type: Rumbalara Reserve

rainforest track right (arrow indicates Henry Parry Drive), down the stairs, past the old picnic area and into the thick jungle like forest. Continue until you reach the intersection signposted Rainforest Track. Turn left and follow the arrow down the metal staircase toward Henry Parry Drive.

Follow the management track again from the staircase and eventually past the Cappers Gully Reserve plaque. At the next intersection, behind the radio station, turn left and follow the bush track as it makes it way to the information board at the intersection of Frederick St and Henry Parry Drive. Follow Henry Parry Drive uphill and turn left at White Street. Pass the Rumbalara Reserve signpost past the gate and continue toward Cappers Gully as signed. At the next intersection turn right and follow the Ouraka Point arrow up the stairs. Cross the foot bridges and climb up through the forest. There are many steps in this area.

At the intersection to the Rainforest Track, turn left. *Do not follow the Bay View Avenue sign.* From the next intersection, follow the walk as directed toward the picnic areas, shortly afterwards coming to the sculpture of Charles Sturt and the halfway mark of the walk.

From the sculpture of Charles Sturt, continue along the management trail to the intersection with the Casuarina Track. Veer right and leave the Casuarina Trak behind as you make your way uphill to the signposted Flannel Flower Track, turn right and follow this track downhill and further along toward the Yaruga Picnic Area. At the picnic area, pass the information board and follow the 'Lookout' sign, turning left at the barbeques and crossing the picnic area towards the road. Descend the stairs and follow the road to the right downhill to the intersection with the bush track on the left. Follow the bush trail past the boulder and downhill to the management track where you turn left. Follow the management track and just prior to the steep downhill, veer left.

You will cross under some power lines and come to a road intersection. Follow the Yaruga Picnic Area arrow and cross the road, through the carpark and onto the Ironbark Loop Track with directions to Nurrunga

Picnic Area. Eventually the Ironbark Loop Track skirts the Nurrunga Picnic area and arrives at the Sir Charles Kingsford Smith Sculpture. It's a short walk from here to the next sculpture on the route. Walk across the picnic ground, behind the sculpture of Sir Kingsford Smith and onto the bush track that leaves the area. You will arrive at the intersection with a sculpture of Matthew Flinders. This is the junction of the Ironbark, Casuarina and Flannel Flowers Walking Tracks.

Follow the Casuarina Track, and at the next intersection follow the Ironbark Loop sign toward the Flannel Flower track arrow. At the next junction, follow the direction arrow for Ouraka Point. At the fork, take the right option and descend the paved steps until you reach the management track. Veer right and continue along the management track downhill until you arrive at the sculpture of Charles Sturt. Continue straight until you come to the signposted Ouraka Point. Ouraka Point is a lookout with commanding views across Gosford and surrounds.

From Ouraka Point, follow down the paved steps and continue straight, crossing the bottom of the management track and descending the metal stairs, some more steps in sandstone and to another intersection. Continue straight again, following the management trail downhill to the information board. Turn right, down the steps and then down the metal staircase to the junction with another management trail. Turn right and at the bottom of the hill take the unmarked track with the wooden steps to the left. Follow this track, down and over a small bridge to the back of the Environmental Education Centre and where you started the walk.

Along the Way:

Rumbalara Environmental Education Centre provides students, teachers and community of the central coast with field work and learning opportunities and has easy access to the landscapes and habitats of the Rumbalara Reserve.

A diverse range of flora and fauna find sanctuary in Rumbalara Reserve. The landscape supports a range of vegetation including Coastal Narrabeen Ironbark Forest and Coastal Warm Temperate Rainforest. As such the birdlife and Wildlife supported in the area is just as diverse. Eastern Rosellas, Glossy Black Cockatoos, Swift Parrots, an array of lizards and even tree snakes can be spotted along the trails.

The Cappers Gully Quarry remains sit in stark contrast to the bushland around it. The quarry features neat squarely cut walls, shapes rarely found in nature.

Yaruga Picnic Area provides facilities for a mid-way picnic and great lookouts across Gosford and the surrounding waters.

The Sydney Flannel Flowers, from which the Flannel Flower Track is named, are spectacular in spring and feature a flannel like texture to their petals.

The bronzed sculptures in Rumbalara Reserve are part of a commission titled 'Salute to Famous Australians' which marked the state bicentennial celebrations in 1987. Featured on this walk is Captain Charles Sturt, Sir Charles Kingsford Smith and Matthew Flinders. Edward Eyre is also situated in the reserve past Redgum Lookout.

Bathers Way Coastal Walk

A coastal walk along some of the most picturesque urban coastline in Australia. This walk is the first leg of a southbound journey along the Great North Walk which starts in Newcastle and finishes in Sydney. Included in this stretch is Strzelecki Scenic Lookout, a great vantage point to spot dolphins frolicking or whales migrating, the Bogey Hole rock pool, with a rich history, the Newcastle Memorial Walk paying homage to our servicemen and women and the picturesque and relaxing King Edward Park.

Description: Starting at Nobbys Beach SLSC, make your way east and then south on the path parallel to Shortland Esplanade and to the Newcastle Ocean baths. Continue along the pathway, past the kiosk at Newcastle Beach, keeping the ocean on your left. Bogey Hole is worth sitting at for a while. Not much further on, signs direct you to Strzelecki Scenic Lookout. This is a great viewing point for dolphin pods year round and the migrating Southern Right Whales between May and November. The Newcastle Memorial Walk is next on the journey and links the Strzelecki Scenic Lookout with another stunning viewing point at North Gilmore Cove via a 160-metre-long bridge.

Now called the Yuelarbah Walk, the path then hugs Memorial Drive and passes by Bar Beach, heading past Dixon Park Beach and progressing to the surf club at Merewether Beach.

Retrace your steps to return to the start.

Along the Way:
Constructed to commemorate the 100th anniversary of ANZACs landing

in Gallipoli, honouring the sacrifices of Australian soldiers and marking the commencement of steel making in Newcastle, the Anzac Memorial Walk memorialises the sacrifices and ingenuity of the people of the Hunter region. The walkway features almost 11,000 names of men and women from the Hunter Valley who enlisted to serve in World War I as well as some silhouettes of soldiers cast in steel with an ocean backdrop.

Dolphins can often been seen frolicking and feeding behind the waves at the beaches and at times diving in and out of the waves. Small sections of turbulent water and sea bird interest in an area can often indicate schools of fish and dolphins may be seen feeding nearby.

The Bogey Hole, once known as Commandants Baths was hand built in 1819 by convicts for the personal use of Major James Morriset. The baths were renamed to Bogey Hole, meaning 'to bathe' in Dharawal.

Closest Town: Newcastle

Start Location: Nobbys Beach Surf Lifesaving Club, corner of Shortland Esplanade and Nobbys Road, Newcastle East.

Latitude and longitude: 32.924630°S, 151.791636°E

Grade: 2

Trail Quality: Paved, some steps, clearly signed.

Distance: 11 km

Time: 3 hours

Amenities: Yes

Park Type: Urban Walk

Merewether Beach

N

600 m

Tilligerry Peninsula Circuit

Taking in the many reserves and parks of the Tilligerry Peninsula, this walk is on flat gradient and the scenery is ever changing. Sea birds are almost guaranteed to delight and the Mangrove Walk is a great place to look out for crustaceans and other sea life. A visit to Tiligerry habitat could mean some time viewing Koalas and a pleasant break from walking.

Description: Make your way through Gibber Point Reserve and follow the formed track in the direction of Lemon Tree Passage, keeping the water on your right. You pass through Mungarra Reserve and then stay right and make your way onto the Lilli Pilli Walkway. Continue along until you reach Nyrang Reserve. Hug the waters edge and make your way along the Mangrove Boardwalk through Koala Reserve with Tilligerry Creek on your right.

At the end of Koala reserve, you will see the Marina ahead on your right. Continue to and past the marina and along the waterfront to Kooindah

Closest Town: Tanilba Bay / Lemon Tree Passage

Start Location: At the corner of Daniel Crescent and Gibbers Drive, Lemon Tree Passage.

Latitude and longitude: 32.739705°S, 152.022769°E

Grade: 3

Trail Quality: Bush tracks, sand, paved areas and some boardwalk.

Distance: 12 km

Time: 3 hours 30 minutes

Amenities: Not at the start, however amenities are available nearby at Lemon Tree Passage or Tanilba Reserve

Park Type: Peninsula Circuit passing through reserves and parks along the waterfront.

Park and on to Rudd Reserve. Through the next section on to Mallabula, the route hugs the shoreline and there is some walking that turns to ankle deep wading in high tide, adding to the adventure.

From Mallabula, the walk continues along the shoreline and onto the Tanilba Bay Boardwalk. The boardwalk passes by Rookes Reserve and Tilligerry Habitat and finishes at Peace Park where a bike track continues the journey.

From here it is some street walking back to the start. From Peace Avenue, turn left onto Avenue of the Allies, left onto King Albert Avenue, and at the roundabout take the trail to the right. Do not take the entry road to the Tilligerry Habitat. This trail passes through Tilligerry Habitat but is not the main trail to the information centre. As you exit the bushland of the Tilligerry Habitat, continue straight along Brittania Drive and Hartford Street, turning right onto Wychewood avenue and left onto Strathmore Road. As Strathmore Road turns 90 degrees to the left, look right and follow the track between the houses and the sports fields. This track winds left and Lemon Tree Passage Rd is on your right. Continue until you come to Daniel Crescent and the finish of the walk.

Along the Way:

Tilligerry Habitat is a 9-hectare reserve on the banks of Tanilba Bay. The habitat houses an abundance of fauna, with a koala and wildlife habitat and has a native nursery brimming with native flora. There is a visitors centre armed with a myriad of information and interactive displays for the curious visitor.

If you are keen to extend your walk, the Tilligerry Habitat offers a 2-kilometre walk on their interior network of paths and boardwalks through some diverse landscape including wetlands and coastal environments. It is possible to see a koala or two in the trees in this area.

Tomaree Head Summit and Fort Tomaree Walk

A serious uphill walk with the rewards matching the effort to get there. Tomaree Heads summit viewing platforms offer unparalleled views of the Port Stephens coastline. The north platform looks out over Cabbage Tree Island, Tacaaba Head and Boondelbah and Broughton Islands while the south platform delights with beach views including Zenith Beach, Box Beach and Wreck Beach. Point Stephens Lighthouse and Fingal Head are also easily spotted. On the way back down a short detour takes you along the Fort Tomaree Walk to military relics from World War II.

Description: From Zenith Beach carpark, head along the paved pathway and begin the climb up the Tomaree Summit track. The track is consistently uphill all the way to the top. The surrounding forest lines the trail and provides ample shade on a sunny day and views of the blue waters of Shoal Bay peak through the trees as you continue to climb.

Closest Town: Shoal Bay

Start Location: Zenith Beach carpark, Shoal Bay Road, Shoal Bay.

Latitude and longitude: 32.718318°S, 152.182851°E

Grade: 5

Trail Quality: The Summit Walk is on formed track, many steps, very steep and at times difficult. The Fort Tomaree Walk is on formed track and is of gentle gradient. Well signposted.

Distance: 3.2 km

Time: 2 hours 30 minutes

Amenities: Yes, 350m west of the start near the boat ramp

Park Type: Tomaree National Park

650 metres into the walk, the trail meets a junction indicating Fort Tomaree to the left and Tomaree Summit on the right. Staying right, continue the remaining 350 metres, which includes some staircases to the summit boardwalks of Tomaree Heads.

On the summit there are several viewing vantage points that take in the vast and rugged and yet serene stretch of coastline.

After basking in the glory of conquering the Tomaree Heads summit, return down the path you came, turning right at the junction

Tomaree Track

Tomaree Head
Gun Emplacement

Tomaree Head Track

Shoal Bay

Tomaree
Lookout

N

200 m

to Fort Tomaree. This route is 550 metres and circles the hillside on fairly flat pathway.

Fort Tomaree has some information boards loaded with information on the history of the area, including the gun emplacements which were part of Australia's military defences between 1942 and 1945.

Along the Way:

Tomaree Heads Summit site 162 metres above sea level. Views stretch across the ocean to Cabbage Tree Island and Boondelbah Island, both of which provide sanctuary and nesting from September annually for Gould's petrel, an endangered sea bird.

The gun emplacements were erected in the defence of the Williamstown aerodrome and the steelworks in Newcastle, both of which were essential to the war efforts in the 1940s.

Tomaree Heads provides a great viewing point for dolphins that can at times be spotted off the coast, you will need some binoculars to view them from the summit.

Tamboi Walking Track

A picturesque walk skirting the edge of Bombah Broadwater and leading onto Tamboi picnic area. This is an easy walk in a naturally beautiful setting along a flat and wide section of track. The Tamboi Walking Track spoils walkers with a diverse forest of cabbage palms, paperbarks and swamp mahogany which appear in abundance along the side of the trail. The walk gives opportunity to take a picnic lunch and enjoy it at the Tamboi Picnic Ground before returning.

Description: From Mungo Brush campground, make your way south to the Tamboi Walking Track head. The trail leads into the bush and is wide and flat and an easy walk. As you meander along, the waterways peak in through the foliage in places and the birdsong of Whistling Kites keeps you company from high above.

Tamboi Picnic Area is on the edge of the Myall River. Across the river is the historic and preserved Tamboi fishing village. The picnic grounds here lend themselves to relaxing and are a great place to enjoy a lunch before exploring the area and retracing your steps back to Mulga Brush Campground the way you came.

Closest Town: Hawks Nest

Start Location: Mungo Brush campground, off Mungo Brush Road, Mungo Brush.

Latitude and longitude: 32.543260°S, 152.308195°E

Grade: 3

Trail Quality: Formed wide track, mostly flat, signposted.

Distance: 5.6 km

Time: 2 hours 30 minutes

Amenities: Yes, at the start

Park Type: Myall Lakes National Park

Along the Way:

Cabbage Palms – these unmistakable palms are one of Australia's tallest native plants standing up to 30 metres high. Their glossy leaves can span up to 4 metres in diameter and they can be found in rain forested sections on the east coast of New South Wales.

The Yellow-Tailed Black Cockatoos are a constant at the Tamboi picnic ground, enjoying the fruits of he She-Oak trees.

The Tamboi fishing village sits across the waters from Tamboi picnic ground on the edge of the tannin-stained water. There are shanty homes, and the village are best accessed by boat.

Yacaaba Headland Walking Track

A beach walk along the pristine waters of Bennett's Beach leads to a challenging bushwalk up and through the diverse bushland on Yacaaba Headland. This walk is all about the views and include landmarks in every direction, from Seal Rocks to Shoal Bay, Port Stephens and on a clear day, Barrington Tops. This walk is much quieter than some of the traditional tourist routes.

Description: Best described as a walk with three sections of very different terrain, the Yacaaba Headland Walk sets off from the carpark at Jimmys Beach Reserve along Bennetts Beach toward the Yacaaba headland.

The first section is a beach walk along Yacaaba Spit and covers 1.7 km along the sand. The beach is picturesque, and it feels like a grand way to start a journey. At the end of the beach there are signs indicating the Yacaaba Headland Walk. There are two options here – take the right fork towards Jimmys Beach Track Lookout.

The second section of this walk makes its way off the beach and into the bush along groomed trail. Heading uphill for the first few hundred metres, the thick vegetation is diverse with some plots of ferns scattered among more traditional beach bushland. The trail rises gentle then flattens off keeping the walk at a steady pace. This section finishes at the Jimmys Beach Track Lookout which looks back over Jimmy's and Bennetts Beaches, and at the peak of Tomaree Head. The views here are stunning and worthy of a postcard. After taking your fill, return to the top of the fork and take the left option.

The last part of the walk is on a much rougher section of trail. It is 500 metres to the summit of Yacaaba Headland and there are rocks, washouts and tree roots to navigate for a good portion of that. While challenging, it is not too hard if you are

Closest Town: Hawks Nest

Start Location: Jimmy's Beach Reserve carpark, end of Beach Road, Hawks Nest.

Latitude and longitude: 32.681101°S, 152.184654°E

Grade: 4

Trail Quality: Formed track, some obstacles, many steps, very steep. Signposted.

Distance: 7 km

Time: 3 hours 30 minutes

Amenities: None at the start

Park Type: Myall Lake National Park

Jimmys Beach Trail

Myall Lake National Park

Yacaaba Headland
Walking Track

N

400 m

happy to slow down and pick the best route for your ability. Once within 100 metres of the summit, the track clears and its an easy jaunt to the top.

The views on the summit are nicely framed by the natural and wild bushland and make for some stunning photographs. The views are multi directional and include Tomaree Head, Shoal Bay, Seal Rocks, Cabbage Tree Island and the many beaches, headlands and bays in between.

Along the Way:

This walk is all about the views. On a clear day you can see the distant ridgeline of Barrington Tops Range.

Angophoras, Banksias and Grass trees are plentiful along the bush section of the walk.

John Gould Nature Reserve sits on Cabbage Tree Island which can be viewed from the summit. The reserve is a refuge for Gould's Petrel, one of the rarest sea birds in the world.

Booti Hill and Wallis Lake Walking Track

A walk that brings the pleasures of the ocean, the rainforest and the precious waters of Wallis Lake together. While the walk can be completed in under 3hours, this walk is well worth setting a day aside and exploring some of the great places along the way. At first smell of the subtropical rainforest, you will instantly feel relaxed. Follow it up with a dip at Elizabeth Beach and relax in the picnic area before exploring the waterside of Wallis Lake.

Description: Leaving the Ruins Campground, follow the signs to Seven Mile Beach and then follow the signs uphill toward Elizabeth Beach. Start the first climb up the steps on the northern side of Booti Hill. The trail is steep and passes through scrubby bush however there are benches along the way to take a rest on. The trail rolls along on a gentler incline and enters subtropical rainforest where you will find yourself amongst a vast array of ferns and strangler figs.

Just after some clear views of picturesque Seagull Point, the track emerges

on the ridge above Lindeman's Cove. Continue until you reach the signs to the trail indicating Elizabeth Beach. It is a steep hike down to Elizabeth Beach but worthwhile. Ignore a turn off to the right.

After a break and swim at Elizabeth Beach, return up the steep trail and to the previous intersection and turn left towards The Lakes Way. Take care as you cross The Lakes Way and into the Lakeside Track, then turn right. This part of the walk is the easiest, with all the hills behind you, you can enjoy the serene views across the water as you meander back to The Ruins Campground.

Closest Town: Forster

Start Location: Ruins Campground, Ruins Camp Road, Booti Booti. Off The Lakes Way

Latitude and Longitude: 32.3106063°S, 152.5195221°E

Grade: 3

Trail Quality: Formed track, some obstacles, short steep hills, many steps. Signposted.

Distance: 7.3 km

Time: 3 hours

Park Type: Booti Booti National Park

Along the Way:

The lookouts make great viewing points for whales migrating during the winter months. It's a good idea to bring binoculars if you are keen on spotting whales.

Elizabeth beach is a great family friendly beach and the only patrolled beach in the area. It is midway through the walk and a great place to spend a few hours.

Wallis Lake is one of the cleanest lakes in Australia. It is 25 km long and 9 km wide. Water flows from the Wallamba, Wallingat, Coolongolook and Wang Wauk rivers into the lake. Having an average depth of 5ft, Wallis Lake is the ideal place for water sports including kayaking, stand up paddle boarding and swimming.

Booti Booti is habitat to an abundance of bird life with over 200 bird species finding refuge in the park. Sea birds such as the endangered little tern and Pelicans are plentiful in the area.

In a grassy clearing just prior the Ruins Campground, the Gogerly Family are buried here in marked graves. The Gogerly's were a pioneer fishing family who once owned the land where The Ruins Campground now sits.

Antarctic Beech Forest Walking Track

The Antarctic Beech Forest Walking Track leads through some of the most pristine Gondwana era rainforest in Australia. Travel through sub alpine woodlands dotted with snow gums before entering below the Antarctic Beech canopy and the enchanting world of the cool temperate rainforest. From mossy carpeted grounds to a myriad of fern species, the rainforest provides crisp respite from the outside world.

Description: Leaving the carpark, after 100 metres you will be presented with two options. The Long Trail which takes around 90 minutes or the Short Trail which takes under 30 minutes. For this walk we take the long trail, although depending upon your schedule – the short trail may be more suitable.

As you step through the rainforest, under the canopy of ancient Antarctic Beech, it is easy to muse about the comparatively short period, humans are

Closest Town: Gloucester

Start Location: Antarctic Beech Forest Carpark, Gloucester Tops Road, Gloucester Tops. It is 56 km from Gloucester via the Bucketts Way.

Latitude and longitude: 32.089608°S, 151.594208°E

Grade: 3

Trail Quality: Formed track, steep in sections, lots of steps, obstacles underfoot.

Distance: 2.5 km

Time: 1 hour 30 minutes

Amenities: None at the start. There are toilets at Gloucester Tops picnic area, 800m away

Park Type: Barrington Tops National Park

on the earth. Some of the trees in this area are thought to be in excess of 600 years old. If only the branches could talk. In the presence of such ancient forest, the experience feels extremely special.

The trail is narrow in places and winds gently through the rainforest and over the rock steps and a creek crossing. Be careful as you walk this area as some of the foot pads are loose.

The next part of the walk is spectacular, the trail descends and sounds of the waterfall makes itself known well before you can see it. As the waterfall comes into sight, you are treated to a three-tiered waterfall surrounded by the greenest of moss and the tallest of tree ferns. Onwards the walk ascends steeply for approximately 500 metres.

There are two main junctions in the latter stage of the walk, continue straight at each junction and back to the carpark.

Along the Way:

The Antarctic Beech Forest is part of the Gondwana Rainforests, an ancient rainforest from over 550 million years ago when Australia and the Antarctic were one body of land. This area of the Barrington Tops is World Heritage listed.

Bountiful in resources, The Barrington Tops National Park is the traditional land several Aboriginal groups, the Worimi, Biripi and Wonnarua people and the Gringai Clan.

River Walking Track

Through diverse forest of Snow and Mountain gums, the River Walking track enters the shallow valley from the Antarctic Beech Forest walking track and makes its way down to and along the Gloucester River. This walk will delight bird watchers and those with a keen eye as the changing details in the environment are intriguing. The riverside is a great spot for a break and picnic as well to observe the local wombats and kangaroos as they go about their daily routines.

Description: The River Walk is a clearly signposted walk, starting at the Antarctic Beech Forest Carpark. Follow the signs into the valley. There are changing landscapes along the way and as you enter and exit various tree canopies, the undergrowth proves just as enchanting with a full canvas of colours as the wildflowers bloom in spring. Continue over the creek crossing and make your way along the Gloucester River. There are plenty of places to stop and observe the fauna around you which are known to include wombats, Grey Kangaroos and Red-Necked Wallabies. Birdlife is also plentiful in this area.

Closest Town: Gloucester

Start Location: Antarctic Beech Forest Carpark, Gloucester Tops Road, Gloucester Tops. It is 56 km from Gloucester via the Bucketts Way.

Latitude and longitude: 32.089608°S, 151.594208°E

Grade: 4

Trail Quality: Gentle Hills, rough underfoot, many obstacles, some steps. Clearly signposted.

Distance: 3.3 km

Time: 2 hours

Amenities: At Gloucester Tops picnic area, 2.5 km into the walk

Park Type: Barrington Tops National Park

Continue along the marked trail to the Gloucester Tops Picnic Area. From the picnic area, turn left onto the Gloucester Tops Road, and walk 800 metres back to the Antarctic Beech Forest Carpark.

Along the Way:

The valley in which the Gloucester River flows is bountiful with wildflowers such as triggerplants, rice flowers, billy buttons, and bluebells during spring.

The ever-cool waters of the Gloucester River are a great spot to put your feet in the water on hotter days.

200 m

Gloucester Tops Rd

Blue Mountains

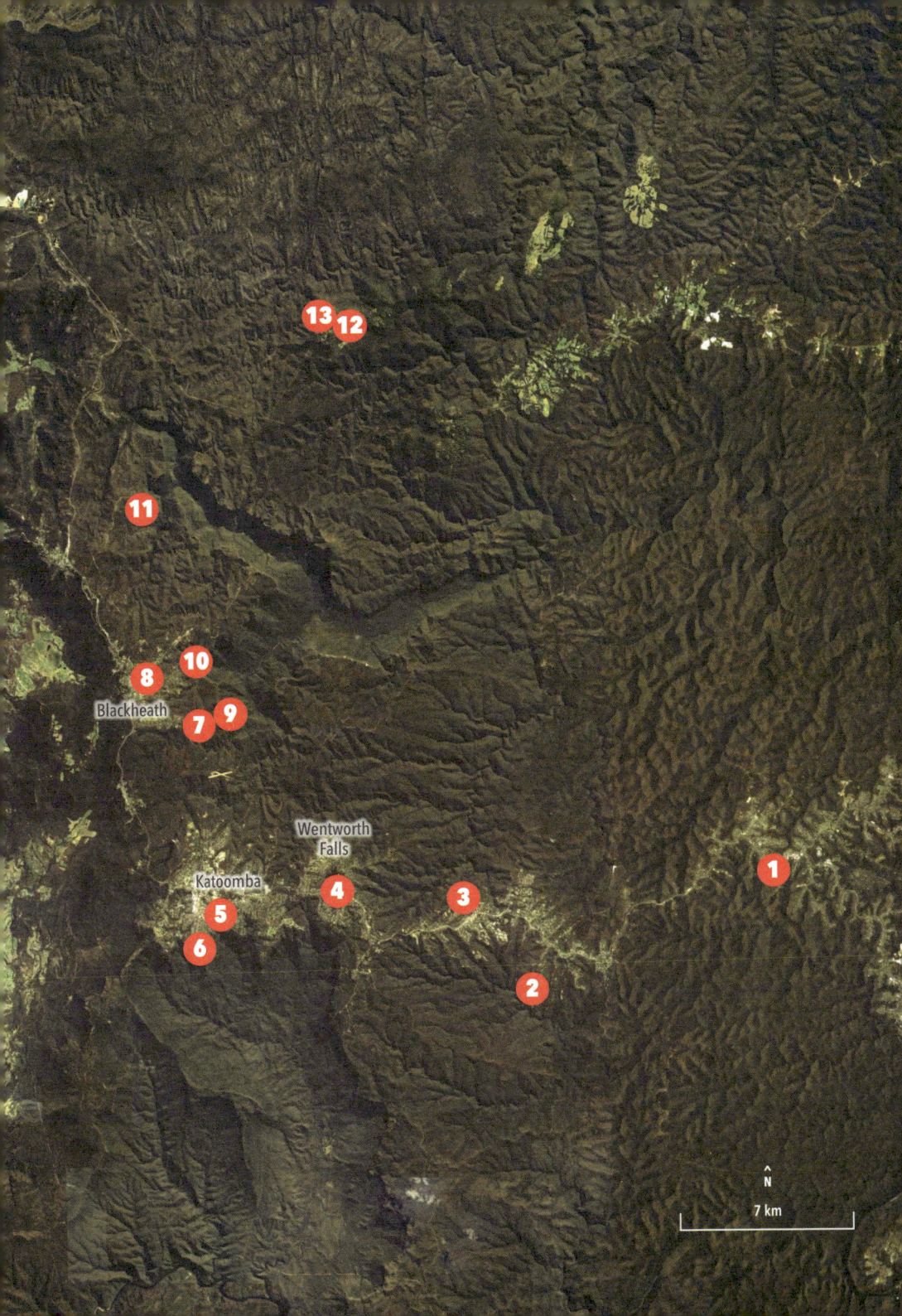

Sassafras Creek

Description: After parking on Sassafras Gully Road, walk to the end of the road and to the left, beside the fence of the last house. The trail tracks downhill to an unsigned intersection with the Victory Track coming in from your right. Turn left here and continue downhill and into the gully. The route continues along the creek, crossing several times. There are tracks coming in from the left at times, including Wiggins Track, ignore them and continue down the gully with the creek by your side. Follow the directions of the Perch Pond signs. The track leaves the creek side on a few occasions, passes through an informal campground and over some hilly sections before continuing downstream.

The approach to Perch Pond Campsite is marked some rocky overhangs and the campsite is located at the meeting of two creeks, providing a small, shaded clearing to relax.

Leaving Perch Ponds, follow the Magdala-Fairy Dell directions as signposted. The track climbs uphill to a small side track leading to Martins Falls. Turn right to visit the quirky Martins Falls. The falls has a trail that leads under a rock overhang behind the waters of the falls. Retrace your steps back onto to the main trail and turn right. Follow the trail up to the Magdala Falls sign and from the intersection continue straight and uphill. The track crosses the creek and there are arrows engraved into the rocks. Turn left here and continue on. The track crosses over and back along the creek before coming to a large rock shelf, and the sign to Lawsons Lookout. Lawsons Lookout offers a filtered view from a large rock shelf across the Magdala Creek valley. Retrace your steps and turn right back onto the main trail.

Follow the trail to the intersection of the Fairy Dell and Picnic Point

Closest Town: Springwood

Start location: End of Sassafras Gully Road, Springwood, off Valley Road. The last house on Sassafrass Gully Road is number 18.

Latitude and longitude: 33.704415°S, 150.557786°E

Grade: 4

Trail Quality: Rough with obstacles, water crossings, steep in places. Limited signage.

Distance: 9.6 km

Time: 3 hours 45 minutes

Amenities: No

Park: Blue Mountains National Park

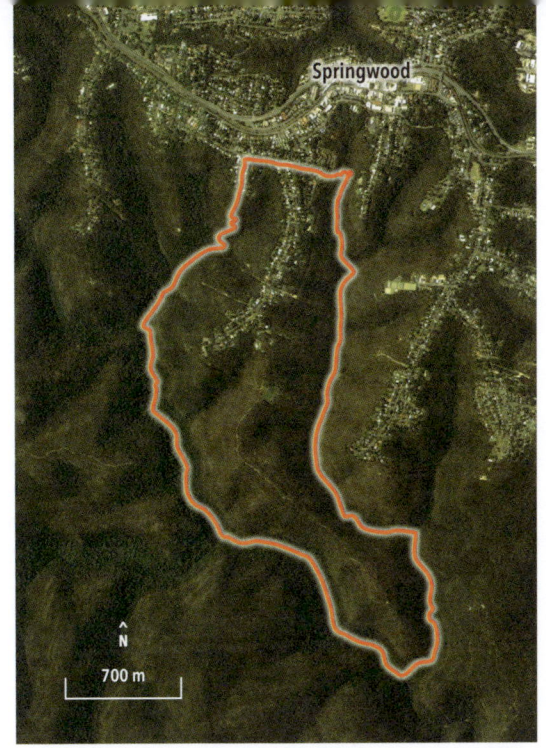

Tracks. Turn left and cross the small bridge to Picnic Point. Make your way across Picnic Point Reserve out to Valley Road and along to Sassafras Gully Road on your left and the finish of the walk.

Along the Way:
Lyrebirds are plentiful along the track and are often seen busying themselves in the lush undergrowth. They appear to be unperturbed by company and this gives a great opportunity to observe them doing their thing.

Perch Ponds campsite is a small unfacilitated campsite with walk in access only. It is close the Perch Pond which at the junction of the Glenbrook and Magdala Creeks and an excellent place to swim on a hot day.

Martin Falls provides a unique experience of being able to scramble in behind the falls and look out through the water curtain.

Tour of Terrace Falls Reserve

The most underrated reserve in the Blue Mountains, Terrace Falls Reserve sports a variety of waterfalls, all with unique characteristics and some sublime swimming holes to dip your toes in. The reserve is dog friendly and the tracks fluctuate between being smooth and wide and, at times, narrow and challenging. There are some great places to picnic, birdwatch, take photographs and swim.

Description: This walk, while it travels a few main trails, has many optional side trips. Notes on the side trips are in the section at the bottom.

From the carpark, start along the fire trail, the first intersection is 200 metres in. (Side trip: Bedford Creek). Take the right turn (Side Trip: Pyramid Falls), passing the track to Pyramid Falls on your left. Continue on to the sign indicating Bedford Pools on your left. (Side trip: Bedford Pools). Continue along to the sign indicating Terrace Falls and Victor Falls and along the track, passing Salote Pool and continue uphill until you reach the spectacular and aptly named Terrace Falls.

Closest Town: Hazelbrook

Start Location: Parking is at the intersection of Valley Road and Terrace Falls Road, Hazelbrook. The starting fire trail is marked with a sign for Terrace Falls Walking Track.

Latitude and longitude: 33.746185°S, 150.454337°E

Grade: 4

Trail Quality: Some smooth wide fire trail, some narrow, rocky and rough trail with obstacles and steps. Signposted.

Distance: 4.7 km

Time: 2 hours 20 minutes

Amenities: No

Park Type: Terrace Falls Reserve

After leaving Terrace Falls, continue along the track to the side track to Victor Falls on your right. (side trip: Victor Falls). Not far after the Victor Falls track junction there is an intersection with the fire trail. Turn right and walk for approximately 1.4 km until you reach the carpark and the finish of the walk.

Along the Way:

Side Trips: Bedford Creek is a relatively unexciting side trip compared to what you are about to experience along the trail. However, all running waterways have their charms and this one is no different.

Pyramid Falls only runs after rainfall and although small, it is a beautiful waterfall with a few spots to sit and contemplate.

Bedford Pools is a fantastic swimming location and has its own sandy beach. It is at a wide part of the creek and there are steppingstones to help you across. The ponds are inviting and there is plenty of room if you have company.

Terrace Falls is perfectly named. The water descends the terraced rocks into the pond below forming an almost perfect picture. There are plenty of opportunities for stunning photographs around these falls.

Victor Falls is probably the tallest of the falls in the reserve. It appears to have several levels and is a cascading fall. It is hard to see the whole falls unless you walk further up the track where you get a better scope of the size of the falls.

Fairy Falls, Dante's Glen, St Michael's Falls and Frederica Falls

North Lawson plays host to some of the best small waterfalls in the Blue Mountains. The trails are rich in flora and the birdlife is diverse. Summer is a great time to walk this circuit and enjoy a swim at one of the many waterfalls or waterholes along the way. Finish in North Lawson Park and enjoy a picnic in this often-quiet reserve.

Description: From the carpark at North Lawson Park, cross the park up the centre and pick up the signposted Dantes Glen Track. The track descends some steps and continues straight ahead. You will pass a sign to Fairy Falls on the right, ignore this for now and continue straight to Dantes Glen. From here continue on the main track along the creek surrounded by ferns and wandering waters, turning right and crossing the creek and stepping stones to St Michaels Falls.

Continue along Dantes Glen Track and as you meet a fork in the track, turn left and join the Empire Pass Track. This track continues along the

Closest Town: Lawson

Start Location: North Lawson Park, end of St Bernards Drive, Lawson.

Latitude and longitude: 33.713718°S, 150.426481°E

Grade: 4

Trail Quality: Narrow trail, many steps, steep in parts, slippery underfoot at times. Mostly signposted.

Distance: 5.7 km

Time: 2 hours 30 minutes

Amenities: No

Park Type: Blue Mountain National Park and North Lawson Park

valley floor beside the creek, sometimes past large boulders covered with moss and at other times on flat and leaf littered soft trail. Empire Pass area is impressive, the colours, sounds and sights along the trail are peaceful and relaxing. Empire Pass Track loops around the valley coming to Frederica Falls.

After leaving Frederica Falls behind, you come to an intersection, turn right onto North Lawson Fire Trail. Follow the fire trail up the hill to the locked gate. At the locked gate take the footpad to your right as it leads into the bushland. At the next junction, turn left and make your way along Empire Pass Walking Track toward Fairy Falls. The trail is beautiful single trail the gully below is rich in flora. At the next intersection, again turn left and continue to Fairy Falls.

Fairy Falls should be crossed with caution as the rocks are at times slippery. Cross the rocks at the bottom of the falls and continue along the track, turning left and making your way up the steps to North Lawson Reserve and the finish of the walk.

Along the Way:

As you come to Dantes Glen, you will be surprised at the untouched paradise feel of this waterfall, the waters tumble off the rock walls and into the small but sublime pool at the bottom.

St Michaels Falls is sublime, the jagged sandstone walls hold onto their ferny housemates with vigor and the waters tumble seemingly carefree over the edge to the small pool below.

Frederica Falls are a cascading waterfall, with each rock platform feeding the next and the water filling a pool that appeared to be a little deeper than the previous falls.

Fairy Falls sport dark red rocks and water tumbles over the rock ledge above before sliding across the rocks, off the edge and down into the valley.

Charles Darwin Walk

Although not the first to make his way along Jamieson Creek to the grand views and waterfalls of the expansive Jamieson Valley, Charles Darwin's awe inspired descriptions certainly encouraged many to walk in his footsteps. In 1836, a young Charles Darwin made his way from Weatherboard Inn to Wentworth Falls via the Jamieson Creek in what was likely a challenging muddy and wet footed walk. 'One stands on the brink of a vast precipice and below one sees a grand bay or gulf... thickly covered with forest', he later wrote.

In modern times walkers can follow the sounds of the water along groomed trails and formed board walk, through hanging swamps and past idyllic homes of green frogs and giant dragonflies to the cascading waters of Wentworth Falls as they tumble freely hundreds of metres into the Jamieson Valley.

Description: Starting at Wilson Park, the modern walk begins through the Grand Entrance marked 'Charles Darwin Walk'. The walk is easy to follow and on a combination of groomed trail and board walk. At some points there are stones across the water to void wet feet, however during summer you may be tempted by the crystal-clear waters to remove your shoes and cool off.

Closest Town: Wentworth Falls

Start Location: Park in the street at Wilson Park on Falls Road, Wentworth Falls.

Latitude and longitude: 33.71107°S, 150.37348°E

Grade: 3

Trail Quality: Easy walk, some steps and obstacles, mainly groomed trail. Signposted.

Distance: 6.2 km return

Time: 3 hours

Amenities: Yes

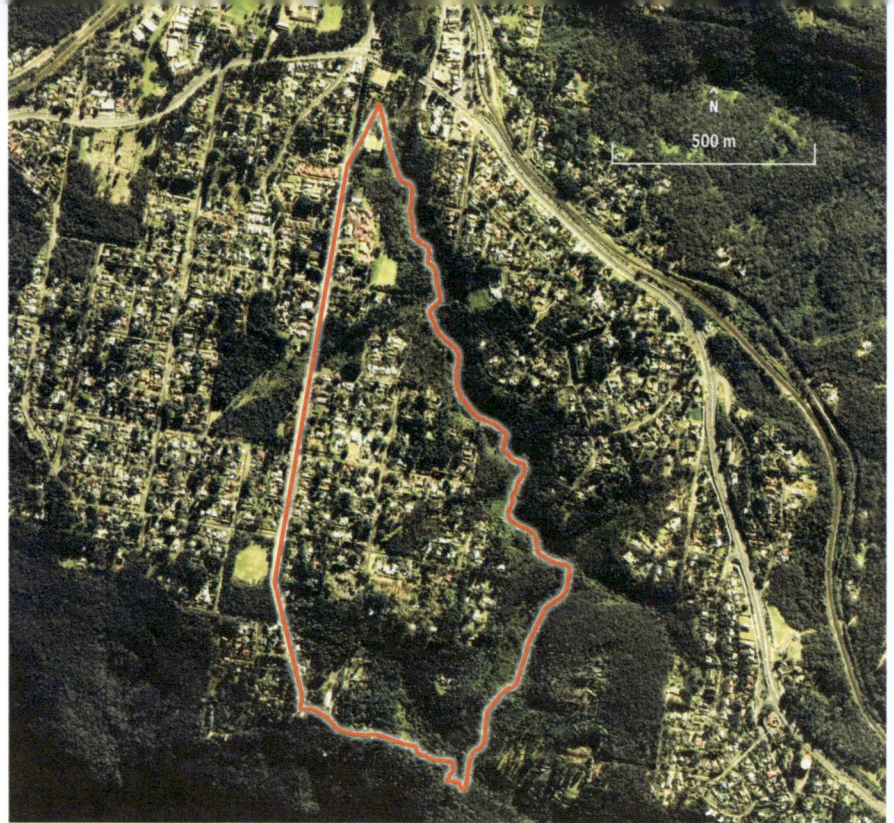

Interesting points along the way include what is there: the hanging swamps and cool waters of the Jamieson creek and what may be there: perhaps some of the ancient crayfish have made their way onto the boardwalk or the Yellow-Tailed Black Cockatoos are feasting in the tree tops or perhaps an endangered Blue Mountains Water Skink makes an appearance. The diverse nature of the flora and fauna along the Charles Darwin Walk ensures no two walks will be the same.

After walking 2 km, you will come to a fork in the track. To the right is the picnic area, where you can find amenities and water. The picnic area also has great viewing platforms and information boards. It is suggested you continue to the left and visit the picnic area on the way back. The track to the left leads to the bottom of Weeping Rock and then on to the top of Wentworth Falls where the waters topple carelessly into the valley. The area is amply signposted.

Return via your route or follow the signs back to the picnic area, and then take Falls Rd back to Wilson Park and the start of the walk.

Along the Way:

Halfway along the track, the path climbs down and crosses the creek via a dam wall. It passes the foundations of what was the dressing sheds for the swimming baths which were built in the nineteenth century.

Prior to reaching Weeping Rock the creek flows beneath a large sandstone overhang. Opposite is a wooden seat offering a place to sit, rest and take in the surroundings. The seat is known as Effies Seat and is in memory of a young woman who died prematurely. A tiny plaque at the base of the seat reads 'In Memory of Effie 25–8–86 A Loved Place'.

In 1986, a commemorative plaque was attached above the path just before the 'immense gulf unexpectedly opens through the trees'. The aging plaque is still there and reads: 'Charles Darwin passed this way in 1836, remembered by his friends in 1986'.

Keep a lookout for crayfish who have been known to make their way from the creek bed onto the boardwalk.

The Blue Mountain Water Skink and Giant Dragonfly, both endangered find refuge in this area.

The birdlife in the area is plentiful and diverse. Yellow-Tailed Black Cockatoos can often be heard and sightings are not uncommon while Honeyeaters are drawn to the nectar-rich banksias.

Leura Cascades Fern Bower Circuit

A scenic circuit with unlimited opportunities for bird watchers and those who enjoy vast and elevated views. Follow the sounds of the flowing waters of Leura Falls Creek deep into the rainforest and toward the cliff edges of the Jamison Valley. This challenging walk is rewarding at every turn with views, wildlife sightings and what appears to be unlimited bird life to observe.

Description: Starting in the popular Leura Cascades Picnic Area, walk under the stone arch and descend alongside Leura Falls Creek following the sound of the trickling waters. Immediately surrounded by rainforest, continue across the foot bridge at Prince Henry Cliff Walk and turn right downstream. The next part of the walk is a scenic circuit with unlimited opportunities for bird watchers and those who enjoy vast and elevated views.

Closest Town: Leura

Start Location: Leura Cascades Picnic Area. Access is off Cliff Drive, Leura.

Latitude and longitude: 33.71934°S, 150.32215°E

Grade: 4

Trail Quality: The track is well formed however there are very steep areas and lots of steps to navigate. There are some underfoot obstacles in places ad uneven ground. The track is often wet and access should be checked prior to leaving in wet weather conditions.

Distance: 4.5 km

Time: 3 hours

Amenities: Yes

Park Type: Blue Mountains National Park

As you reach the Bridal Veil Falls lookout, the views into the Jamison Valley reveal themselves. This is a great place to take in the fresh mountain air and the serenity of the valley below.

Ascend the steps along the western cliff line and on the Round Track, after approximately 100m turn left onto the Amphitheatre Track. The track then descends steeply into the rainforest, follow the track for another 100m, ascend some steep stairs and then traverse the half-way ledge and into a natural amphitheatre. Continue along this ledge on the track and you will come to the intersecting Fern Bower

Track, ascend the stairs here back to the Prince Henry Cliff Walk. Turn right onto Prince Henry Cliff Walk and follow the track to the foot bridge you crossed earlier in the walk. Turn left and return to Leura Cascades Picnic Area. This walk is well signposted and easy to follow.

Along the Way:

The sound of water rushing over mossy rocks and through untouched rainforest combined with the many and varied surrounding bird songs create a calming and peaceful walking experience.

Rock formations and overhangs are plentiful along the Prince Henry Cliff Track.

Bridal Veil Falls Lookout is stunning and breath taking all at once.

At the end of the walk, Leura Cascades Picnic Area provides as good a place as you will find for a picnic afterwards and well-earned rest.

The Best of Katoomba

With one of the most complex and historic trail networks in Australia, Katoomba is host to some amazing bushwalking. This walk links several iconic trails together for an exceptional walking experience. Visit the Three Sisters, Echo Point Lookout, Katoomba Falls, Furber Steps, The Giant Stairway and a multitude of lookouts and great views along the way. This walk captures the best of the Katoomba trails in the Blue Mountains National Park. A challenging walk with well over 1800 steps, descending into and out of the iconic Jamison Valley.

Description: Starting at Echo Point, make your way down to the viewing platform and take in the fresh surrounds of the Jamison Valley with views to Mount Solitary. As you approach the viewing platform there is a ramp on your right leading down onto Prince Henry Cliff Walk.

Follow Prince Henry Cliff Walk along the top of the cliffs to Lady Darley Lookout, Cliff View Lookout and on to Kedumba Creek past the spectacular Katoomba Cascades. After the falls you come to an intersection with the Round Walk (also known as Furber Steps Track). Continue straight, leaving Prince Henry Cliff Walk and making your way onto the Round Walk. There

Closest Town: Katoomba

Start Location: Echo Point, corner of Cliff Drive and Echo Point Road, Katoomba.

Latitude and longitude: 33.731509°S, 150.311952°E

Grade: 4

Trail Quality: Challenging with many uneven steps, ladder style steps and bush tracks. Obstacles underfoot. Clearly signposted.

Distance: 6 km

Time: 3 hours 45 minutes

Amenities: Yes, at the start

are several intersections in a very short span. Follow the signs and start to descend Furber Steps.

Descend the steps past Queen Victoria Lookout and continue downwards into the valley. You soon come down metal steps towards Federal Pass. At the bottom, turn left onto Federal Pass.

Federal Pass takes you through lush rainforest areas teaming with tall ferns and thick undergrowth. You are now walking in the direction of Echo Point. Follow Federal Pass until you come to a split in the track with Dardanelles Pass Walking Track. Veer left onto Dardanelles Pass Walking Track and walk up to the next intersection with the Giant Stairway on the left. Time to start climbing.

Climb the Giant Stairway up past the iconic Three Sisters rock formations until you come to the Three Sisters Walking Track under the arch. Follow this track, up past the information centre to Echo Point and the end of the walk.

Along the Way:

The Three Sisters – Subject of several Dreamtimes stories, this iconic rock formation is an important part of Aboriginal legend. While the stories are

varied, the ending of both stories is similar with the three sisters Meehni, Wimlah and Gunnedoo being turned to stone to protect them from evil and remaining as stone due to the witchdoctor being unable to undo said spell. Whatever legend says, these sandstone formations stand proudly looking across to Mount Solitary and the wilderness beyond.

Federal Pass – Built in 1900, originally connecting Leura Forest with Katoomba Falls and onward to what became known as the landslide area. The pass was extended in 1936 out to the Ruined Castle and now forms part of the Mount Solitary Loop.

Furber Steps – Securing a government grant for 140 pounds led to Furber Steps being constructed to replace a precarious set of poles steps leading to federal pass.

The Giant Stairway – Chief Ranger of the area, Jim McKay conceived the idea of a giant stairway that would link Echo Point area with Federal Pass via Dardanelles Pass. 1916 saw the start and finish of the project as costs and difficulty proved too steep to overcome. In 1932 work was recommenced and the project this time was successful leading to the 998-step masterpiece that is the Giant Stairway.

Evans Lookout to Govetts Leap

To the left, windswept health and hanging swamps don the escarpment. To the right, the great expanse of the Grose Valley and mountains beyond enchant the imagination. As you walk along the cliff top trail towards Govetts Leap, the views and surroundings seem to change between steps. From gazing over the edge into the ancient forests of the Grose Valley to close up views of water freefalling to the valley floor. Your attention is constantly drawn to the small details in the vast expanse. The flora that clings haphazardly to the nooks of the sandstone cliffs and ledges to the scurrying water dragons crossing the trail on a mission, this is an exciting, stimulating and thought provoking walk.

Description: From the noticeboards at the Evans Lookout Carpark, walk back toward the amenities and pic up the trail as it leads off toward your right and the clifftop. Follow the trail downwards as it makes its way through dense windswept heath and past hanging swampland, both teaming with wildlife and rare flora. The Along the clifftop you can look up the neck of the Grose Valley toward Mt Banks and Mt Tomah. Lockleys Pilon can be seen on the far banks of the valley.

Closest Town: Blackheath

Start Location: Evans Lookout Carpark, Evans lookout Rd, Blackheath.

Latitude and longitude: 33.64659°S, 150.32514°E

Grade: 3

Trail Quality: Formed trail, lots of steps, boardwalk and some underfoot obstacles. Signposted.

Distance: 6.2 km

Time: 2 hours 30 mins

Amenities: Yes, at the start and finish

Park Type: Blue Mountains National Park

The heath comes alive during spring with wildflowers and birdlife, including the white-napped honeyeater which is lured with the promise of nectar.

As you pass over the boardwalk at Haywards Gully, the swamp below provides haven for all manner of skinks and dragon lizards and they are regularly spotted on a mission across the boardwalk. There are

seats along the way to sit and enjoy a break or the views or both.

Barrows Lookout provides another aspect to the vast views of the Grose Valley. Cross Govetts Leap Brook and start the ascent to Govetts Leap lookout. The view from Barrows Lookout is world class, both into the distance and immediately in front of you.

At Govetts Leap there is a picnic area, amenities and place to rest. The lookout here allows you to look back along the track toward Evans Lookout and view Bridal Veil Falls.

Return to Evans Lookout via the same route.

Along the Way:

Prior to setting out from Evans Lookout carpark, it is worth a walk out to both Valley View Lookout and Evans Lookout to soak in the views and align yourself with the magnificence of the inspiring Grose Valley. Directions for both are at the track head information boards at the end of the carpark.

Waterfalls are easily viewed at Barrows Lookout. These can be viewed again at Govetts Leap.

The hanging swamp in the Barrows Lookout area is home to the rare plant known as Fletcher's drumsticks. Fletchers Drumsticks is only known to grow in the Blackheath area.

Govetts Leap to Pulpit Rock Walk

You would be forgiven if you snuck a glance over the edge at Govetts Leap lookout and instead sat the walk out in favour of staring aimlessly into the vast gap that is the Grose Valley. However many treasures and many more gasps of awe await you as you make the walk along the rim of the Grose Valley and to the intriguing Pulpit Rock Lookout. Starting at the startlingly beautiful and vast lookout of Govetts Leap, walkers hug the clifftop and make their way along the rim of the Grose Valley to Pulpit Rock. Pulpit Rock is on an isolated pinnacle, the rock is a unique shape and juts out and into the Grose Valley. An exposed walk with an ever-changing landscape and views.

Description: Govetts Leap is a perfect launch pad for this walk with what would surely be a top 10 view in Australia.

The track begins to the left of the Govetts Leap Lookout. Make your way down the steps and into the shelter of a stand of black wattle trees. The track crosses the bridge and starts to follow the cliff edge. There are multiple small lookouts as you make your way along the cliff top. The views along the clifftop span 280 degrees and take in both the valley floor, the sandstone cliffs surrounding the valley and the mountains atop the plateau and into the distance.

Park Type: Blue Mountains National Park

Closest Town: Blackheath

Start Location: Govetts Leap lookout, end of Govetts Leap Road, Blackheath.

Latitude and longitude: 33.62813°S, 150.31129°E

Grade: 3

Trail Quality: Formed track, lots of steps. Gentle inclines. Can be challenging in places. Signposted.

Amenities: Yes, at the start and finish.

Crossing Popes Glen Creek, steps lead up to the lookout above Horseshoe Falls and then continue further along the cliff line. Travelling through open heathland and past hanging swamps, the terrain is interesting and diverse. As you round the bend and get the first sighting of Pulpit Rock, the eucalypt forests feature and there is a short walk with some steps out onto Pulpit

Rock. It is advised to set some time in your schedule to spend at Pulpit Rock, from here there are commanding views of Mt Banks to the left and across the valley on top of the cliffs, Lockleys Pilon sits neatly, appearing like a small pyramid on the plateau.

Retrace your steps to return to Govetts Leap.

Along the Way:

The Clifftops and valleys around Blackheath are a haven for many threatened and rare species of Flora. The Blue Mountains cliff mallee tree can be found on some of the most exposed cliff edges. Fauna sightings such as the rare giant dragonfly with a wing span of up to 12.5cm makes its appearance around October annually and the Australia's largest native slug, the red triangle slug could be prominent on rainy days closer to the Fairfax Track.

The National Parks and Wildlife Visitors Centre, at the gate that leads to Govetts Leap Picnic Area. The visitors centre staff are knowledgeable about the local area and there are displays that detail information and history of the surrounding parks. Light refreshments are available for purchase along with great reference books and souvenirs.

Grand Canyon Loop

With trails in the area since 1907, the Grand Canyon track sits comfortably in its own perfection. Located below rugged sandstone cliffs and deep in the abundant and rich surrounds of the Grose Valley, this walk imparts the gravitas of the landscape perfectly.

Description: The track head at Neates Glen carpark is well signposted and tracks immediately downhill on what will be the first of many steps. The trail makes its way from the dry forested area into the lush rainforest, marked with ferns and mossy rocks and the gorge walls rise dramatically.

The track loosely follows Greaves Creek and even if it is out of sight, if you stand still, you can hear the trickling waters. As you come to the junction at the sandstone cliff, turn right and continue.

Once under the tree canopy, the next part of the walk through the Grand Canyon is exciting. The sandstone stepping stones characterfully pave the way as they have for over a century, carrying the ambition of travellers from all over the world through the wonderous canyon. The trail winds around, under overhangs and past ancient trees covered with vines. The lighting is different down here and there are plenty of ferns and mossy rocks and the smells of the rainforest are strong and fresh and wise.

Continue through the Canyon and to the climb out to Evans Lookout. The track is steep and climbs up some well-formed sandstone steps. It is clearly signposted and easily followed. There are railings to help you along your trip and once you reach Evans Lookout, the carpark has amenities and information boards about the area.

From Evans Lookout carpark, it

Park Type: Blue Mountain National Park

Closest Town: Blackheath

Start Location: Neates Glen Carpark, opposite 216 Evans Lookout Road, Blackheath.

Latitude and longitude: 33.651433°S, 150.314666°E

Grade: 3

Trail Quality: Steep, formed trail with lots of steps. Well maintained and clearly signposted.

Distance: 5.9 km

Time: 3 hours 30 minutes

Amenities: None at the start – there are amenities at Evans Lookout, 4.3 km into the walk.

is a short walk along the roadside trail to Neates Glen carpark and the end of the walk.

Along the Way:

The view from Evans Lookout is brilliant during sunset. The last light casts onto the sandstone cliff walls, and the spectrum of colours through orange, yellow and red are on full display creating an enchanting scene. Evans Lookout views stretch up the Gross Valley toward Mount Banks.

Sydneysiders have made their way into the Blue Mountains since the 1800s. There was believed to be natural remedy in the fresh mountain air and by the early 1900s tourists from afar began to travel into the area. In 1907 the Grand Canyon Track was built and has been maintained meticulously since.

Lyrebirds, mostly oblivious to their human visitors, are plentiful along this track, the busy environment provides a thick and prosperous undergrowth for them to rake and scavenge through.

Popes Glen to Govetts Leap, Fairfax Track

Starting at the endearing Duck Pond in the township of Blackheath, a short street walk links walkers with the Popes Glen walking track which traverses Popes Glen Creek Valley, bringing walkers to the cliffs edge and the coveted Grose Valley. Passing a beach, pagoda and waterfalls, the big prize of this walk is the humbling views of the Upper Grose Valley from Govetts Leap. Return via the Fairfax Track

Description: From the parking spot at the Duck Pond, follow Prince Edward Street around to the right and onto Wills St and then Dell St. After walking along Dell Street look out for a sign on your right which indicates the start if the Popes Glen Track.

Angling down into the Popes Glen valley, the track follows the creek

Country: Dharug and Gundungurra

Closest Town: Blackheath

Start Location: The Duck Pond, Prince Edward St, Blackheath.

Latitude and longitude: 33.63426°S, 150.29073°E

Grade: 3

Trail Quality: The trail can be narrow in the Popes Glen valley. It is well signposted however expect obstacles underfoot. Prior to and along the cliff top, the trail can be rough, steep in parts and at times eroded depending upon recent weather events. The Fairfax track is paved and pram friendly.

Distance: 7.4 km

Time: 3 hours

Amenities: Yes

Park Type: Blue Mountains National Park

between residential properties and through a ferny understory. There are several side tracks to be ignored as the track continues in a downhill direction. After approximately 500m the track crosses over the creek on a small bridge and continues. Within the next 600m there are several cross tracks and intersections that led up to residential streets. Continue downward at each intersection ignoring the side tracks. The track crosses the creek on a number of bridges and continues until you reach a signposted track junction. Popes Glen track continues on as signposted however the side track here leads on a short diversion to Boyds Beach, a small sandy area on the side of a paddle worthy pool in the creek.

Making your way back to the Popes Glen track and continue as signposted toward Govetts Leap – The last section of Popes Glen Track includes viewing an impressing pagoda and small waterfall before reaching the junction with Pulpit Rock Track. At the junction turn right and follow the sign directions toward Govetts Leap. The track climbs steeply out of the Popes Glen Creek Valley and on to the cliff top. The track can be rough underfoot and caution should be taken in the next kilometre.

Once on the cliff top, the views of the upper Grose Valley are enchanting and there are a number of lookouts to stop and view the deep valleys below.

The signposted turn to the right is the easiest way to reach Govetts Leap where commanding views await.

The next leg of the walk takes in the Fairfax Track.

From Govetts Leap Walk uphill past the amenities and join the Fairfax Track on the right as it leads into the bushland. Walk past the hanging swamp and on to George Phillips Lookout, with commanding views of Mount Hay across the Grose Valley. Pass landmarks such as Sunshine Bay, Waratah Rest and Cone Stick Corner as you reach the hollowed-out base of the intriguing Scribby Gum Tree. A tall stand of Grass Trees indicate the trail is soon to emerge at The Blue Mountains Heritage Centre. From here it is a street walk up Govetts Leap Road to Prince Edward Street. Turn right onto Prince Edward street and walk downhill to the Duck pond and the finish.

Along the Way:

Blue Mountains Heritage Centre – Located at the entrance to Govetts Leap, and at the top of the Fairfax Walk, the centre staff are knowledgeable about the local area. There are displays detailing information and history of the surrounding parks. Light refreshments are available for purchase along with great reference books and souvenirs.

Boyds Beach – a sandy spot just off Popes Glen Track. Great place to rest, paddle and keep cool on a summers day.

The unique Pagoda rock formation on Popes Glen Track overlooking Popes Glen creek.

Views into the Grose Valley and home of the Blue Gum forest and what is believed to be Australia's first big conservation test. In 1931 a group of Sydney bushwalkers visiting the Blue Gum Forest, a unique stand of trees in the Grose Valley below Govetts leap, were made aware of a farmer's proposal to cut all the trees down for a walnut farm. Within 3 months the group had formed the Blue Gum Forest Committee, Australia's first conservation action group. A price of 130 pounds was negotiated with the farmer to purchase his lease and after public appeal and some generous loans, the land was purchased in 1932. The committee donated the land back to the government as a reserve for public recreation. The Blue Gum Forest was preserved and continues to be revered and protected.

Plant life along the Fairfax Track is intriguing with Grass Trees (*xanthorrhoeas*), Scribbly Gums and Persoonia of Geebung Grove.

Victoria Falls

A short but steep walk rewards with the magnificent Victoria Falls and the often photographed Silver Cascades. Silver Cascades is reached after only a few minutes on the trails and is a great spot for a swim or picnic. Victoria Falls is at the bottom of an often-steep trail with some magnificent flora on display. The track passes along some ledges which sit above some drops into the valley and is narrow in places. This is a great walk if you are looking for a day out, spend some of the time walking and the rest swimming and relaxing.

Description: Starting in the Victoria Falls carpark, follow the signposts for 150 metres to the lookout over Victoria Creek and the upper Grose Valley. The Victoria Falls are not yet visible; however the panoramic view of the valley is spectacular.

Leaving the lookout behind, the track starts to make its way downwards, cutting back and forth, making its way under small cliff faces, over wooden steps and down some steep sections, eventually coming to Victoria Creek. The signs here indicate Burra Korain Flat to the left and Cascades to the right.

Closest Town: Mt Victoria

Start Location: Carpark at the end of Victoria Falls Road, Mt Victoria. It is a 5 km drive along 2wd quality dirt road.

Latitude and longitude: 33.573693°S, 150.291154°E

Grade: 4

Trail Quality: Formed Track, some obstacles under foot, many steps, very steep. Signposted

Distance: 4 km

Time: 2 hours 30 minutes

Amenities: No

Park Type: Blue Mountains National Park

The Cascades option takes you along to Silver Cascades, a small detour to a picturesque set of cascading waters as they tumble over the rocks into a large and enticing pool.

The Burra Korain Flat option continues along the left side of Victoria Creek and makes its way to the bottom of Victoria Falls. Victoria Falls has a drop of 20 metres, sending waters hurtling across the rock overhang and into the serene pool at the bottom. Water from here continues into the Grose Valley and

onward eventually to the Nepean River.

After a swim, picnic or relax, retrace your steps up the incline to the carpark.

Along the Way:

Victoria Falls Lookout: viewing the amazing sandstone cliff faces and rugged terrain, from left to right, Asgard Head, Birrawang Walls and Burra Korain Head can all be viewed clearly.

Yellow-Tailed Black Cockatoos make their home high in the trees in this area and are often spotted flying in pairs.

Chinaman's Hat and Pheasants Cave Walk

Vast lookouts into unwalked wilderness, aboriginal markings indicating a bygone culture, cool rainforest bowers, a stream, a cave and a Chinaman's hat... In just 3.7 km this walk packs in great value and experience for the time spent on your feet.

Description: The walk starts and finishes opposite the Mt Wilson rural fire station. Start by walking west down Du Faurs Rocks Road. At the bottom of the road take the signposted turnoff to the Chinaman's Hat Track. This is

a well-formed track and there are spectacular views to the west and into the Wollangambie wilderness.

As you travel, note the Aboriginal markings on the rocks. This is where tools were sharpened, and small grooves were made for water to be collected. Once you reach Chinaman's Hat, the sights and the sounds of the wilderness take over and this is a great place to sit and contemplate.

From here the track leads down the right side of Chinaman's Hat before turning right to Table Top Rock. This turn is easily missed, be sure to pay attention to the arrow on the rock! Tabletop Rock provides another place for respite and contemplation before heading onwards to Du Faurs Rocks Lookout. The track leaves Table Top rock on the right hand side of the ridge above and turns left and then follows the contour lines below Du Faurs Rocks

Closest Town: Mt Wilson

Start Location: Opposite the Rural Fire Service Depot on the corner of Du Faurs Rocks Rd and The Avenue, Mt Wilson.

Latitude and longitude: 33.50547°S, 150.36746°E

Grade: 4

Trail Quality: The main track is well-formed, however there are lots of tracks that lead off the main track and care should be taken at each junction to ensure you are following the route. Caution in wet weather especially along the Pheasants Cave track. Limited signage.

Distance: 3.7 km

Time: 2 Hours

Amenities: No

Park Type: Blue Mountains National Park

lookout before meeting up with Pheasants Cave Track. Pheasants Cave Track is signposted and indicates a 45-minute return walk. It is recommended you allow extra time to soak in the cool bower of the Pheasants Cave area.

A path has been cut into the rocks and the track is well marked however caution should be taken during wet weather as it gets very slippery. Once you reach the stream, cross over and walk to the right. Here the rainforest takes over and water falls over the edge of the rocks. The cave is beyond the falls and is frequented by lyre birds which early explorers mistook as pheasants.

Along the Way:

Chinaman's Hat – A rock formation in the distinct shape of a Chinaman's Hat. As you sit on the top there is a sweeping view into the Wollangambe wilderness. Beneath are caves born from weather events.

Pheasants Cave – Named due to the prominence of lyrebirds in the area which explorers mistook for Pheasants, Pheasants Cave sits snugly behind a waterfall and in a rainforest area. The undergrowth is lush and the temperature moderate on the hottest of days.

Waterfall Walk and Cathedral of Ferns

Combining the tranquillity of the renowned Waterfall Walk with the serenity of the Cathedral of Ferns this is a great walk on a hot day as the rainforest hood and waterfall creek provide cool refuge. Find yourself emersed in a true rainforest experience including sassafras, giant coachwood, tree ferns and corkwood.

Description: This walk is in 3 parts, linking the Waterfall Walk to the Cathedral of Ferns walk.

Part 1: Starting in Waterfall Reserve, and with your back to Chimney Cottage, make your way to the left, across the picnic ground to the track head. The walk down to Waterfall Creek is along a steep but defined track.

Park Type: Blue Mountains National Park

Closest Town: Mt Wilson

Start Location: Waterfall Reserve, end of Waterfall Rd, Mt Wilson.

Latitude and longitude: 33.50814°S, 150.37539°E

Grade: 3

Trail Quality: Waterfall Walk, although on formed track, is steep and narrow in places, it can be slippery when wet. The walk between the reserves is a street walk shared with traffic, proceed with caution. Cathedral of Ferns is a short walk on formed track, some obstacles underfoot on both walks. Signposted in places.

Distance: 5.5 km

Time: 2.5 hours

Amenities: Yes, at the start and finish.

As you approach the creek, the rainforest thickens and you find yourself under a canopy of tree ferns, coachwood and sassafras, the fragrance is strong and fresh.

Making your way along Waterfall Creek, the waterfalls are plentiful and unique, you will encounter mossy rocks with cascading waters, and basalt cliffs with water tumbling down from height. Follow the track as it makes its way back to the picnic area.

Part 2: From the picnic area, it's a 2.1 km stroll along Waterfall Rd, onto Mount Irvine Rd and to the Cathedral Reserve Picnic Ground. Although a quiet road, keep to the verge for safety.

Part 3: As you approach Cathedral

Reserve Picnic Ground, the track head is to at the far end of the reserve and immediately crosses the Mount Irvine Road before re-entering the bush. Walk into the Cathedral of Ferns into what feels like a Jurassic forest where the tree ferns reach the sky. In 2008 lightning strike razed the 'Giant Tree', a *Eucalyptus fastigata* of mammoth proportions. Follow the path up behind the Giant Tree and the path will come out on a track, keep left. Pass through the gate with the hole in it (not the private property gate) and continue to keep left until you return to the picnic ground.

Along the Way:

During autumn when the trees turn the colours at the reserves and along the street walk are spectacular.

A walk as the sun sets may include firefly sightings at Waterfall Reserve.

Central West

Ida Falls

A single trail adventure through a secluded valley, with rocky overhangs and creek crossings – opening onto a spectacular amphitheatre waterfall. Ida Falls is a mesmerising walk in the middle of Lithgow but somehow in the heart of nature.

Description: With an underwhelming urban starting point, the rewards of Ida Falls walk, although hidden to start, become apparent after just 300m. From suburbia to what feels like a long forgotten and untouched secret valley, the Ida falls trail is a single trail surrounded by imposing rock overhangs on the right and impenetrable climbs and sharp bush cliffs on the left. The valley is also home to pristine valley water which snakes its way through to your starting point. Your walk takes you against the flow finishing at the beautiful amphitheatre where the water enters the valley.

Starting with a walk through a turn of the century sandstone viaduct, there is a narrow ledge on the left if you wish to keep your feet dry from the onset. This tunnel is naturally lit and a testament to early century engineering. The walls are rough cut sandstone affording passers-by with a fingerhold and reassurance. If you are lucky, you will hear a train rumble overhead. Emerging from the tunnel you stick to the left of the creek for about 40m before taking a right at the 'yellow arrow'. Walking through an old farm paddock with relics dotting the sides of the trails, your imagination

Park Type: Lithgow City Council

Closest Town: Lithgow 2790

Start Location: From the east end of Main St Lithgow, turn left across the railway bridge and immediately right into Inch St. Follow Inch St to Bells Rd and continue to a small clearing on the right, just past 1 Bells Road. To pick up the trail, locate the railway underpass tunnel, which ferries water from the valley creeks and walk through. Yellow arrows mark the way onto the single trail.

Latitude and longitude: 33.46806°S, 150.18839°E

Grade: 3

Trail Quality: The trail is well established and mostly smooth underfoot with minimal tripping hazards. Creek crossings are of varying width and while some have stepping stones, others will require a decision to either jump or cool your feet in the crystal-clear waters. At most the crossings are ankle deep. Not signposted.

Distance: 4-kilometre return

Time: 2 hours

Amenities: No

threatens to wander into an era bygone. Soon you rise to what is the main elevation of the walk into Ida Falls.

As you enter the canopy of trees you immediately notice the untouched and pristine nature of the surroundings. To the left the hills jut skyward and at certain vantage points you can spot the famous top points station, a stop on the historic zig zag railway.

The trail takes a vantage point a few metres higher than the creek bed and winds along the embankment for the most part on the right side of the creek. Further in, there are both the aforementioned creek crossings and a few short and sharp climbs spanning no more than 20m each that divert you around large trees or difficult rocks. While these diversions can be challenging, they are short and manageable and give you the opportunity to stop, breathe and take in the intensely beautiful surroundings of this hidden gem. Your relatively flat and smooth trail continues after each diversion.

After approximately 1900m the valley turns a bend and Ida Falls appears. Clear freshwater cascades from a height of about 30m, hitting the valley floor in amphitheatre style before narrowing to form the creek you have just followed. This walk gives the impression of seeking and finding the water at its source. With relatively few walkers on route, it is a great place to enjoy a bit of serenity and being so close to urbanisation, it feels like a secret place to visit.

Along the Way:
The historic Top Points Station infrastructure can be spotted at the top of the gully and to the left approximately 800m into the walk.

Hanging swamps and large overhanging rocks don the right side of the trail as you walk further into the valley. Plant life and wildflowers are plentiful.

Interesting brick structures reinforcing the creek remind you that you are not far from civilisation, however, will leave you puzzled as to who knew to come to such a spot with a barrow of bricks and a trowel... it feels unimaginable.

The amphitheatre housing the falls is a great place to sit, contemplate and recharge with some snacks before making your way back along the trail.

Newnes Industrial Ruins

A walk through history, once the site of a thriving oil shale mining industry, the Newnes Industrial Ruins walk is a fascinating walk beneath the high honey coloured sandstone cliffs at the head of the Wolgan Valley. Remarkably well preserved, remnants of a bygone industrial era include brick kilns, old coke ovens, paraffin sheds. This walk gives you an eerie feeling as the evidence of a bustling settlement is now being gradually reclaimed by nature.

Description: Leaving the carpark, cross the river on foot using the steppingstones on your right. At the next junction, turn left and follow the old railway easement for 1 km. You will pass the old railway platform on your left and a junction that leads down to the old cricket ground, also on your left. Mainly used as a camping ground, there are amenities at the old cricket ground if needed. Continue until you reach the Ruins Carpark, and the start of the Ruins walk. There are information boards detailing the history of the ruins.

Closest Town: Lidsdale

Start Location: Park at the junction of Wolgan Road and the river crossing. 250m north of the Newnes Hotel.

Latitude and longitude: 33.177124°S, 150.236175°E

Grade: 3

Trail Quality: River crossing – across stepping stones. Railway easement is smooth and flat. The ruins walk section is a narrow walking track with steps and some obstacles underfoot. Some Signage.

Distance: 4.2 km

Time: 2 hours

Amenities: Yes

Park Type: Wollemi National Park

From the Ruins carpark it is a 2.2 km walk through what was once a thriving industrial site. The industrial township of Newnes mined oil shale at the turn of the century and it was transported out of Newnes by train which ran along the railway easement you walked in on. Remarkably well-preserved remnants of the old brick kilns, coke ovens, oil washing tanks, paraffin sheds and ruined buildings of the old township are slowly being reclaimed by nature but for now provide a great insight into the once bustling and industrious area.

Continue along the route until

you reach the Ruins carpark and then return along the railway easement, turning right to cross the river and back to the carpark.

Along the Way:

At the carpark, notice the large wombat seat. A recent addition to Newnes, it has a plaque and story to tell.

Newnes Railway Platform – The station where the steam locomotive transported supplies and passengers in and out of the valley.

The Old Cricket Ground – Still with a wicket in the middle, now used for camping, this was the site of the townsfolks recreation.

The unique **Beehive Kilns** sit neatly in place over a hundred years after their last use and are the largest of their type in Australia.

A 15m high **retaining wall** sits perfectly preserved in the remote bushland. It is a stark reminder of the scale of the works that took place at the industrial ruins.

Mystery Mountain sits high above on the south side of the trail as you walk along the railway easement.

Newnes

Wollemi National Park

300 m

Glow Worm Tunnel Newnes

A popular track to observe glow worms in their natural habitat, this is an easy walk which can be done with children. The 400-metre-long tunnel was built in the early 1900s to give passage to the steam trains entering the Wolgan Valley to collect resources mined and processed in nearby Newnes. The Tunnel is home to thousands of Glow Worms and is surrounded by lush rainforest and interesting fauna.

Description: From the carpark, follow the signed trail to the Glow Worm Tunnel. You will pass through tall eucalypt forest and narrow rock formations, catching glimpses of the enchanting pagodas along the way. The walk is approximately 1 kilometre until you reach the opening of the tunnel and on a gentle gradient. Before entering the tunnel be sure to have your

Closest Town: Lithgow

Start Location: Glow Worm Tunnel Road Carpark. Starting in Lithgow the route is signposted from the corner of Bridge Street and Main Street. Turn left at Atkinson Street and right at State Mine Gully Road. Continue on Glow Worm Tunnel Road for over 30 km to the carpark, passing through an intermediate tunnel not long before the road ends.

Latitude and longitude: 33.247903°S, 150.223463°E

Grade: 3

Trail Quality: Formed track, some obstacles under foot. A few steps. Can be slippery in the tunnel during rain events when the water is high. Limited signage

Distance: 2 km return

Time: 2 hours

Amenities: No

Park Type: Wollemi National Park

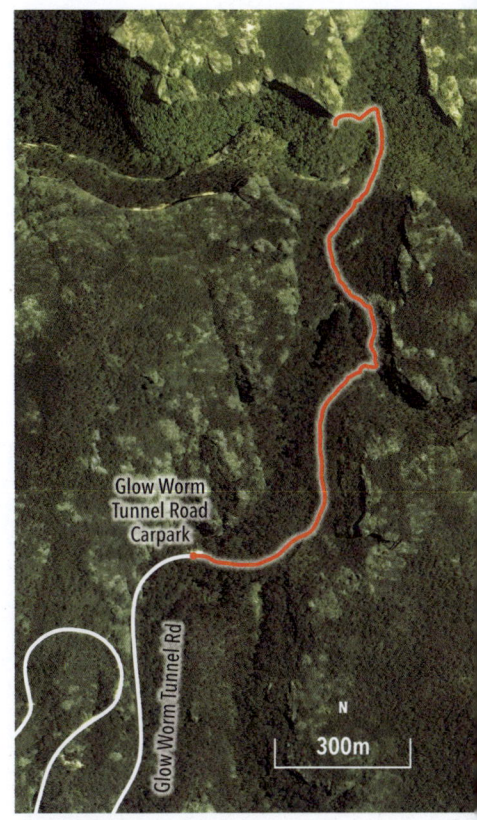

Glow Worm Tunnel Road Carpark

Glow Worm Tunnel Rd

N

300m

light handy and on a cool day, add another layer as the temperature drops sharply in the tunnel.

Upon entering the tunnel, keep noise to a minimum and make your way along the high ground side of the tunnel. You will find there is a natural watercourse that snakes along the floor of the tunnel and the water depth and flow depends entirely on recent rain activity. There is a slight curve to the tunnel and as the light of the entry disappears, turn your light off and wait a few minutes in silence. A brilliant display of small blue lights illuminate the walls and roof of the tunnel giving the illusion of gazing at a starry nightscape.

At you leave the tunnel you will find yourself in lush rainforest with small bridge crossings and a trail that leads down the escarpment toward Newnes (10 km trip). This is a great place for a break and refreshments before retracing your steps back through the tunnel to the carpark.

Along the Way:

Lyrebirds and Goannas are plentiful in his area. Some Wallabies and Koalas may also be spotted.

Stunning Pagoda Rock formations are intriguing and can be seen prior to entering the tunnel. The pagodas are a conical shaped rock formation which is thought to be formed by differential weathering of the sandstone. While there are two types of Pagodas, Smooth pagodas and Platy pagodas, the ones in this area are known as Platy Pagodas which are stepped and terraced and resemble pagodas of the Asian areas. The differential weathering effect is easily observed on the platy pagodas.

Flora includes the yellow pagoda daisies and the ever-enchanting banksias.

Evans Crown Nature Reserve Walk

Self-titled by the inspired Assistant Surveyor George William Evans in 1813, and gazetted as a nature reserve in 1975, Evans Crown Nature Reserve provides spectacular views across 425 hectares. Amongst the reserve, with its diverse flora and fauna sit the impressive and giant Granite Tors. Once amongst the giant tors and their mystic aura, you can envisage why this was a culturally special place of initiations and corrobboree for the Wiradjuri people.

Closest Town: Tarana

Start Location: Located 3 km south/east of Tarana. Access is from Honeysuckle Falls Road off the Lithgow, Tarana, Sodwalls Road. There is an information board at the start of the walking track.

Latitude and longitude: 33.537558°S, 149.932611°E

Grade: 3

Trail Quality: The track is well formed, there are lots of steps in the first kilometre. Obstacles underfoot on the plateau. Some of the side trails you may explore are considerably less formed. You may find yourself climbing on some of the Granite Tors to explore the sights into the distance.

Distance: 2.3 km

Time: 1 – 2 hours depending upon exploration and picnic time.

Amenities: No

Park Type: Evans Crown Nature Reserve

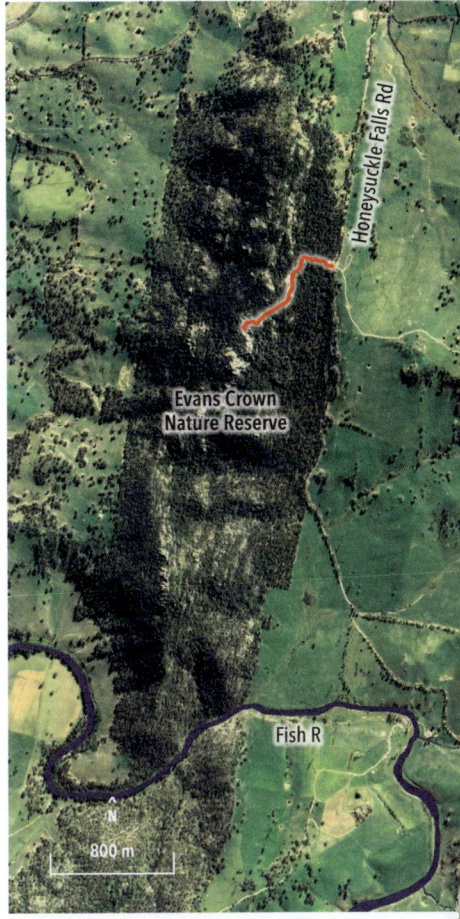

The summit of Evans Crown is 1104 metres elevation and offers an exposed outlook and many amazing spots to picnic. The walk is easily navigated with plenty to explore along the way. There are large sections of rock covered in Lichen, and the different species of lichen form colourful patterns on the rock, once wet they become enchanting to view and photograph.

Description: Starting in the carpark on Honeysuckle Falls Road, an information board details the surrounding area. The trail is a formed pathway and easily followed. In the first 1.1 km the track climbs with lots of steps before making its way around the hillside for the final climb up around and past a mountainous granite boulder onto the plateau. Upon reaching the end of the stepped area, the formed track finishes and the informal trails on the plateau lead left and right with several forks off each of these trails. While the walk to the top takes approximately 45 minutes, once on the plateau, Evan's Crown is intriguing and a great place to spend at least another hour exploring, wandering and relaxing.

There are plenty nooks and rock faces to explore and the lizards scatter as you find yet another vast granite shelf from which to view the valleys below.

There are all manner of natural picnic spots to enjoy and endless places to enjoy the views, granite tors, fauna and flora.

The tors you see on the surface of the landscape began their formation underground, first as molten rock which cooled and eventually cracked and weathered into the shapes you see today. During the formation process, the edges were weathered off, forming 'marble' like shapes and as the earth eroded away, the tors were eventually exposed. Being above ground and exposed to the elements speeds up the weathering process as thin layers of the boulders fall away over the effects of years of wind and rain and sun.

Granite consists of feldspar, mica and sand (silica). The mica and feldspar weather more readily than the silica, leaving the soils in the reserve as sandy and easily eroded.

Fauna – Eastern grey kangaroos are common to the reserve. Less common, the red-necked wallabies, echidnas, wombats, and platypus in waterways may also be sighted. There is also a thriving nocturnal community of rats, sugar gliders possums.

Flora – Reflecting the variation of aspect, slope, elevation and exposure, the flora in the reserve is plentiful and varied. The eastern slopes provide

ideal growing conditions for the Apple Box, Ribbon Gum Green Wattle, bracken and blackthorn. The Northern and Western slopes are home to mountain gum, yellow box, black salt, and blackwood. Snow Gums, known to enjoy extreme conditions, make an appearance around 900 metres elevation.

The lichen which is seen plentifully on the granite tors at Evans Crown have played a large part in the evolution of the shapes of the tors. Algae and fungi which make up 'lichen' have a symbiotic relationship, each relying on the other for survival. The algae, which contains chlorophyll, draws on the suns energy for food, while the fungi forms a protective layer around the algae and provides nutrients and water from its granite host. The result is the addition of a diverse texture and feel to the landscape and a weathering effect for the shapely tors.

McKeown's Valley Walking Track

Known to the local Aboriginal people as Binoomea meaning 'Dark Places', the Caves did not receive their now official title until 1884 when Jenolan, meaning 'High Mountain' was adopted. Jenolan Caves are thought to be over 350 million years old and the oldest limestone caves in the world.

According to legend, James McKeown, namesake of the McKeown's Valley walking track and McKeown's valley was the first to seek refuge in the caves in the Jenolan area. Mr McKeown was an ex-convict and rumoured outlaw and the caves of the karst landscape provided a dry refuge amongst rugged and often impassable bushland. This walk explores the magnificent Devils Coach House Cave and wanders through the karst landscape of McKeown's Valley, which once accommodated the leisure activities of a small population and visitors alike.

Description: Leaving Caves House, walk downhill and pass under the Grand Arch, the track starts to your left. Follow the signboards to and through the Devil's Coach House into the beautiful McKeown's Valley. Remnants of the historic recreation areas still exist including the concrete cricket pitch and

Closest Town: Oberon

Start Location: Jenolan Caves House, 4655 Jenolan Caves Rd, Jenolan NSW 2790.

Latitude and longitude: 33.820155°S, 150.021416°E

Grade: 3

Trail Quality: Formed track, many steps, some obstacles. Clearly signposted.

Distance: 2.6 km

Time: 2 hours

Park Type: Jenolan Karst Conservation Reserve

Amenities: Yes, at Caves House

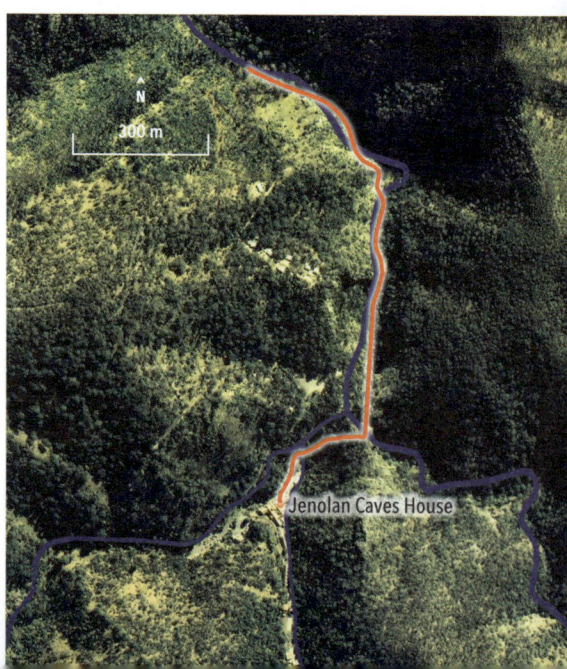

campground. Continue to follow the Valley track as it crosses the Jenolan River, looking into the unique and intriguing blind valley, a landscape feature native to the karst environment. This steep sided, flat-bottomed valley, terminates abruptly and is intriguing to gaze at.

Return via the route you came back to Caves House.

Along the Way:

The area around Jenolan is teeming with wildlife, including rock wallabies, swamp wallabies, lyrebirds who make themselves busy in the undergrowth and goannas sunning themselves.

The Devil's Coach House was named after a reported vision from a camper in McKeown's Valley. The camper reported seeing a ghost like vision of the devil on a horse drawn coach charging through the cavernous archway.

Devils Coach House is a cavernous archway that leads through the mountainside into McKeown's Valley, at its highest point the roof is 57 metres high.

If you want more caves, there are paid guided tours through 11 caves in the area, some of these caverns have hosted musical arrangements and the tours are informative from a geological and historical perspective.

Jenolan River Walking Track

From the Historic Caves House, this walk treats you to the beauty of Blue Lake, a platypus haven. Crossing the Jenolan River, the waters below make their way over intriguing karst waterfalls and into sublime ponds below. Also known as working waters walk, the area is rich in history and leads to the site of the old hydroelectric outfit that powered the Jenolan Caves settlement. While the walk will not take 2 hours, taking in the magnificent surroundings will add to the time you are out on the trail.

Description: Leaving Caves House, walk downhill through the Grand Arch. After crossing under the arch, turn right onto the signposted Jenolan River Walking Track. As you skirt the Blue Lake, be sure to watch quietly for platypus going about their daily work. The Blue Lake has been cordoned off as a swimming location due to its relevance to platypus breeding in the area. Continue along the track, beyond the picturesque weir and through woodland as you follow the Jenolan River downstream. There is a small detour to the swimming hole at the bottom of the small waterfalls. This is a great place for a fresh swim and picnic.

Additional to this walk, continue along the track and down the hillside to the old Jenolan Hydro Electric Power Station. Return the way you came to Caves House.

Closest Town: Oberon

Start Location: Jenolan Caves House, 4655 Jenolan Caves Rd, Jenolan NSW 2790.

Latitude and longitude: 33.820155°S, 150.021416°E

Grade: 3

Trail Quality: Formed pathway, many steps, clearly signposted.

Distance: 2.6 km

Time: 2 hours

Amenities: Yes

Park Type: Jenolan Karst Conservation Reserve

Along the Way:

Blue Lake was originally created in 1908 after Jenolan River was dammed for the purpose of aiding electricity output. Fed by the Jenolan River and the River Styx, Blue Lake is an important breeding ground for the duck-billed platypus in the area.

The amazing blue colour of the water of Blue Lake and the grandiose

nature of Grand Arch make for a spectacular photo when combined.

The Jenolan hydroelectric power station powered lighting in the Caves from 1889. It is known to be the fifth hydroelectric power station of its type in Australia. Prior to the station being built, the caves were lit by battery power.

N

300 m

Jenolan Caves House

Federal Falls Walk

A picturesque loop track taking in the waters of Boree Creek as they tumble down Federal Falls, on the semi alpine slopes of Mt Canobolas. Along the way, the wildflowers are spectacular in spring and the butterflies that make their home among the wildflowers are especially colourful and prolific. There are plenty of vantage points to take great photographs at the bottom of the falls which are best viewed after some rainfall. There are also some great areas to sit and relax before making your way back to the campground.

Description: There are trail heads at the northern and southern end of the Federal Falls campground. Start at the southern end of the campground and walk the loop in a clockwise direction. There is a large information sign at the southern end of the campground which marks the track head.

Closest Town: Orange

Start Location: Federal Falls campground. Once you enter Mount Canobolas State Conservation Area, follow Mount Canobolas Road, then turn right onto Towac Road before the summit. Federal Falls Campground comes up shortly on your right, park and start from here.

Latitude and longitude: 33.349076°S, 148.977517°E

Grade: 3

Trail Quality: Clearly marked, formed track with many steps and some short steep hills. Signposted.

Distance: 4 km

Time: 2 hours

Amenities: Yes, at the Campground

Park Type: Mount Canobolas State Conservation Area.

Meandering along the flat first section of the trail, there soon becomes a gradual descent into the forested area. The wildflowers by the trail in this area are spectacular in springtime. Continue along the trail crossing the creek several times. After 2 km you come to a junction in the track. The options are the Northern Trail to your right or Federal Falls straight ahead. Continue straight ahead.

As you reach the steep descent and the wooden steps, be sure to use the hand railing where it appears for safety as the trail becomes steeper as you descend into the valley. As you descend views of the waterfall appear. Walk a little further and take some time to sit beside the waterfall on one of the many conveniently placed boulders. You can walk further into the base of the waterfalls, just keep in mind the rocks at the bottom can be quite slippery.

To return, retrace your steps out of Federal Falls area and to the previously passed junction with the Northern Track. Continue along the Northern Track, a shorter but uphill track, returning to the campground.

Along the Way:

Once at the waterfall, check out the area behind the waterfall – there is a secret cave there!

Wildflowers are bountiful in spring, including the Australian Pea Flowers and Flag Flowers.

There is plenty of birdlife in this part of the Mount Canobolas State Conservation Area including:

Thornbills, Flame Robins, wrens, currawongs, rosellas, treecreepers, honeyeaters and if you are lucky you may sight the Southern Boobook Owl.

Mt Canobolas Summit and Nature Walk

Make your way from Summit to Summit on this walk, catching the beauty of the Nature Walk on the return trip. This walk combines great views over the city of Orange with an exquisite nature experience. Combined there are over 950 flora and fauna species in the park, which also boasts being home to the only *Eucalyptus canobolensis*, or Silver-leaf Candlebark trees in Australia.

Description: Leaving the Canobolas summit, follow the signs down the steps onto the Summits Walking Track. This track makes its way downhill before reaching the first junction where you turn left, staying on the Summits Walking Track. Continue and at the next junction turn right, again continuing along the Summits Walking Track. A few hundred metres on you will pass two signs to the Nature Walking Track on your right, continue straight ahead – again staying on the Summits Walking Track until you reach the summit of Young Man Canobolas.

After taking in the views of the area, and exploring the rocky outcrops, return along the summits walking track turning left at the first sign indicating the Nature Walking Track. After approximately 1 kilometre there is a small out-and-back section on the nature track that leads to The Walls carpark and onto the Walls Lookout. Return once again to the Nature Walking Track and continue as it loops around, meeting with the Summit Walking Track after 2 km. Turn left onto the Summit Walking Track, stay left at the next junction and right at the following junction.

Closest Town: Orange

Start Location: Mount Canobolas Summit, Mount Canobolas Road, Canobolas.

Latitude and longitude: 33.344067°S, 148.982554°E

Grade: 3

Trail Quality: Formed track, some obstacles, some steps, some inclines. Signposted.

Distance: 4.2 km

Time: 2 hours 45 minutes

Amenities: Yes, at the start and finish

Park Type: Mount Canobolas State Conservation Area.

Along the Way:

Mount Canobolas, once a tyrannical volcano with a rather violent reputation is responsible for the landscape as it is today. The towering basalt cliffs and rocky outcrops, the heaths and forested areas, coupled with the cooler temperatures of the higher altitude have created a haven for a kaleidoscope of flora to flourish.

Traditional land of the Wiradjuri people, 'Canobolas' comes from the words Gaahna Bulla, which in Wiradjuri language means 'two shoulders'. Two shoulders refers to the peaks of Old Man and Young Man Canobolas which sit side by side.

This was an important place for the Wiradjuri people with male initiation ceremonies, traditional tool making and hunting and gathering of food and medicines taking place in the region.

Eucalyptus canobolensis, also known as the Mount Canobolas Candlebark or the Silver-Leaf Candlebark is a threatened species of eucalypt tree native only to the Mount Canobolas area.

Bird watching is special in the park with flame robins, superb fairy wrens, honeyeaters, thornbills and the usual suspects; magpies and kookaburras all making Mount Canobolas their home.

Spring displays of wildflowers see a throng of white, yellow, red and purple flowers light up the heaths. Rare Orchids have been identified in the park, and after the bushfires, two new orchid types were identified and a further two were rediscovered after not having been seen for over 20 years.

Castle Rocks Walk

The sandstone pagodas at the end of the Castle Rocks Walk sit hidden amongst the ensuing bushland, their rugged and layered peaks rising above the tree line haphazardly, just enough to tantalise the curious mind. This walk is flat and easy and the reward at the end is breathtaking views across the Munghorn Gap Nature Reserve. The bushland, a combination of eucalypt and native pine makes for an ideal breeding ground for the plethora of birdlife who make their nests in the tree branches and trunks.

Description: Park at Moolarben picnic area, and walk 1.8 km south along Wollar Road to the Castle Rocks trailhead. (Parking at Castle Rocks trailhead is strictly for 4wds only). The walk into Castle Rocks is flat and on a slightly sandy trail. The bushland is typical for the area and a kaleidoscope of wildflowers are on show during the spring months.

Four kilometres from the trailhead, a sign indicates Castle Rocks is just 150 metres away. Upon reaching Castle Rocks the sandstone pagodas make their peaks known from the tops of the trees below. The pagodas stretch as far as the eye can see and make for a magnificent sight, something akin to a lost city. The best views are from the first rocks you come across at the end of the walking track and there is plenty to explore whilst staying high on the ridge. Be aware that descending from the lookout down and under the tree cover amongst the pagodas it is easy to get lost. The landscapes all look the same from the ground and although the temptation for adventure may be high, there have been many reported lost walkers in the area.

Return the same way.

Closest Town: Mudgee

Start Location: Moolarben Picnic Area, Wollar Road, Munghorn. 38 km northeast of Mudgee.

Latitude and longitude: 32.403584°S, 149.836499°E

Amenities: Yes, bush toilets at the start

Grade: 3

Trail Quality: Formed sandy track, some steps, flat walk until the final rocky lookout. Limited signposts however there is nowhere really to go wrong.

Distance: 12.1 km

Time: 3 hours 30 minutes

Park Type: Munghorn Gap Nature Reserve

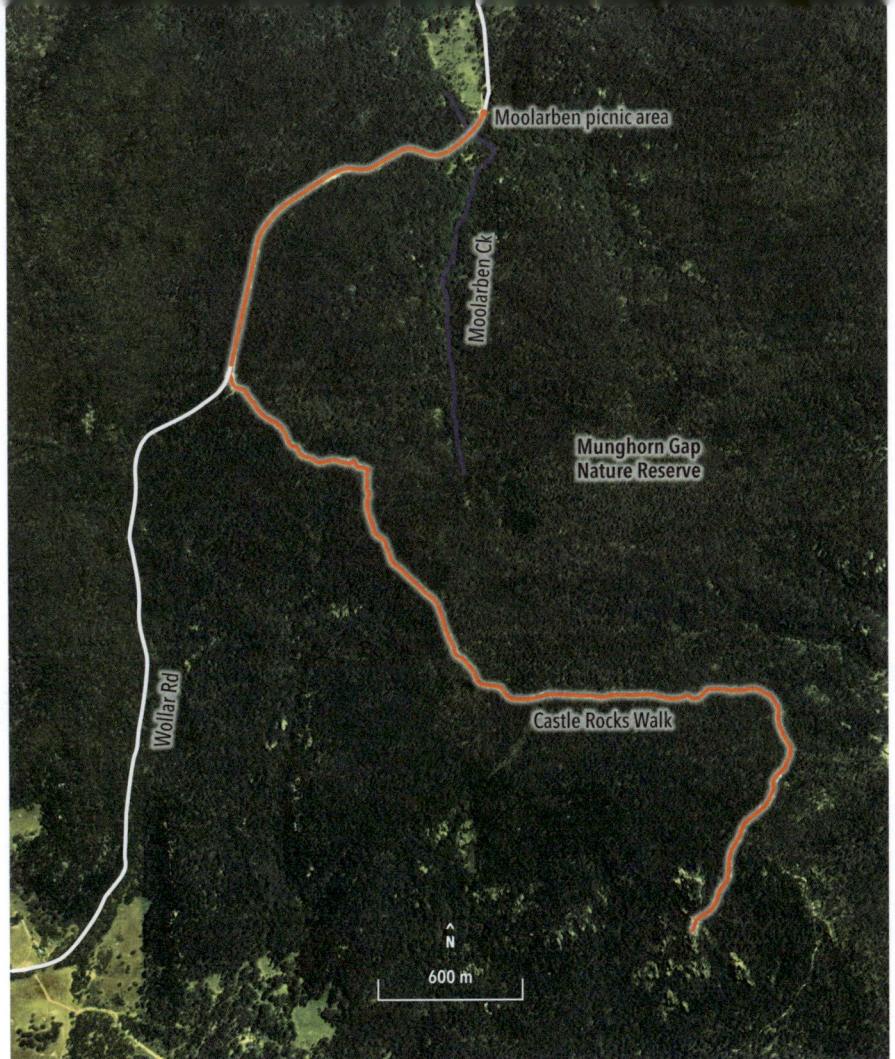

Along the Way:

The second oldest nature reserve in Australia, the area was inhabited by Aboriginal people for over 12,000 years prior to European settlement. A significant place for the Wiradjuri people, Munghorn Gap once served as a trading route between the plains and the blue mountains areas.

Birdlife is plentiful in the area and 164 species of birds have been recorded including the endangered and rare regent honeyeater. Emu also roam the reserve freely. The park has a healthy population of birds of prey including wedge-tailed eagles, peregrine falcons, brown goshawks, whistling kites and collared sparrowhawks.

The Drip Walking Track and The Hands On the Rock Walking Track

With the temperature by the river being some 10 degrees cooler than open area nearby, this is a perfect walk for hot days. The Drip Walking Track hugs the Goulburn River as it makes its way downstream to the 'The Drip' or 'Great Dripping Wall, a large sandstone wall which percolates natural spring water through the rockface. There are plenty of places to stop and enjoy the pristine flowing waters and the sandy bottomed ponds near The Drip are great for a swim. On returning to your car, the nearby Hands on the Rock Walking track offers a great cultural experience before leaving the area.

Description: Leave the carpark and join **The Drip Walking Track** as it makes it way along the left-hand side of the Goulburn River. The cliffs and rocky outcrops rise on your left as you enter the gorge and the trail winds along at an easy pace. From the start of the walk there is plenty to ignite the senses, from the sounds and sights of the pristine waters making their way downstream, to the natural sounds of the birds and wildlife that make their

Closest Town: Mudgee

Start Location: The Drip Gorge carpark, Ulan Road, Ulan. The carpark is 53 km north of Mudgee, on the right just after the road crosses the Goulburn River.

Latitude and longitude: 32.215831°S, 149.787578°E

Grade: 3

Trail Quality: Formed trail, occasional steps, uneven rocks and creek crossings. Handrails in places. Clearly signposted.

Distance: 2.8 km

Time: 2 hours

Amenities: Yes, at the carpark

Park Type: Goulburn River State Conservation Area

homes nearby the flowing water source.

The bushland is a spectacular rich green, with diverse plant life including well established ferns which have wedged themselves into any fertile crack in the landscape. The trail is easily followed and although you are only a few kilometres from the carpark, it feels like you have left civilisation far behind.

As you come to the river crossing there are stones to walk across and it is possible to keep your feet dry. Continue along the trail until you come to a junction, continue straight and you come to a lookout over the Drip Gorge. Retrace your steps to the junction and continue along the main trail into the gorge and to The Drip.

To return, retrace your route back along the river to the carpark.

Hands on the Rock, an Aboriginal rock art site of the Wiradjuri people is only 2 km drive north from The Drip track head. The walk is a short 600 metres each way and brings you to a long sandstone overhang with significant amounts of hand stencils and other aboriginal rock art. Viewing is from behind a fence and there is a clear boardwalk to view from. Information boards give context to the history and cultural significance of the area.

Along the Way:

Diverse and abundant flora line this riverside walk, from orchids and moss hugging rocky outcrops to native apple gums, eucalypts, grevilleas, river oak and a plethora of ferns. The diversity of flora and nourishment attracts a wealth of wildlife and birdlife to the area.

There are clear water ponds along the Goulburn River throughout the walk. These make for enticing spots for swimming or just sitting with your feet in the water.

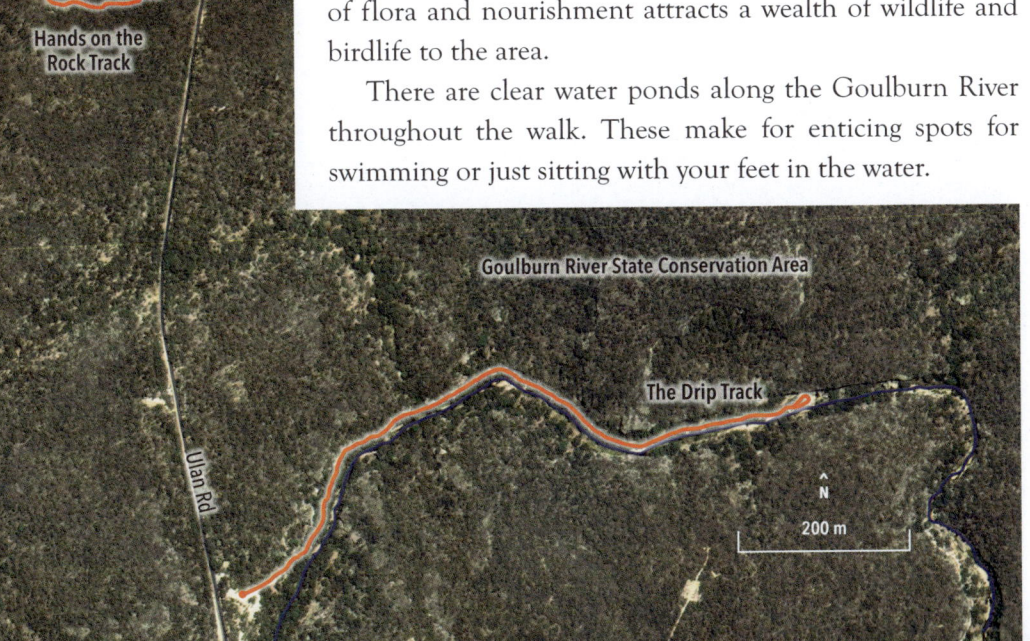

South East

N

60 km

Bittangabee Bay to Green Cape Walking Track

Steeped in history both triumphant and tragic, this walk evokes images of the early settlers and their aspirations and heartbreaks. Some 200 years on and the industry that settled the area is long gone, given way to the frequent walkers, nature lovers and camping enthusiasts.

Description: From the Bittangabee picnic area follow the sign marked 'Camping Area 500m', noting arrow markers as you go. At the next intersection follow the sign for 'walking track' in a downhill direction toward the water. When you reach the roofless building which was once the Bittangabee Bay Store House, locate the information board on the water side of the building.

From the information board, and leaving the Bittangabee Bay Store House ruins behind, the walk leads uphill to an intersection which is signposted and indicates 'walking track', the walk is guided from here with arrow markers indicating direction. The landscape diverges into both melaleuca and low health as the mouth of Bittangabee Bay comes into sight. Reaching the southern edge of the entrance to the bay, a clear view exists to the south, taking in the rugged and picturesque coastline. Glancing down to the pristine blue ocean waters reveals a red rock platform below which contrasts with its surroundings.

Follow the arrow markers around the headland, keeping the ocean on your left. A set of stairs traverse a small creek bed which is often dry and walkers continue upstream meandering within reach of the creek with several more creek crossings and small hill climbs to

Closest Town: Eden

Start Location: Bittangabee picnic area, Bittangabee Bay carpark. Located at Bittangabee Access Road, Bittangabee Bay. Note: There is a fee to use this park.

Latitude and longitude: 37.21676°S, 150.01765°E

Grade: 4

Trail Quality: Overgrown in places, some uneven ground, short rises and narrow trail to navigate.

Distance: 7.5 km

Time: 3 hours one way

Amenities: Available at the start, at 4.6 km and the finish.

Park Type: Ben Boyd National Park

navigate. While some walking takes place on service roads and connecting trails, arrow markers continue to provide walkers with confidence and direction along the way.

A diversion to Pulpit Rock is recommended as you come into the Green Cape Rd carpark at approx. 4.6 km. Follow the stairs which descend from the service track down to Pulpit Rock.

Returning to track, continue to the intersection of the Ly-ee-moon Cemetery. Again a small diversion from the journey seems worthwhile as thoughtful reflection of the lives lost during the 1886 wreck of the Ly-ee-moon is immortalised at this solemn site.

300m on and you arrive at the Green Cape Lighthouse carpark. 300m further on you can explore the historic Green Cape grounds including the telegraph station, lighthouse keepers cottages and if you have timed your walk well, a lighthouse tour.

Along the Way:

Dating back to the late 1870s, the shell of the Bittangabee Bay storehouse remains standing and the concrete foundations of what was once the timber

N
800 m

Bittangabee
picnic area

Bittangabee Rd

Ben Boyd
National Park

Green Cape Lighthouse

Disaster Bay

Bittangabee Wharf are visible. Both structures were built to facilitate the construction of the Green Cape Lighthouse with a wooden tramway built to move construction materials and supplies between the cove of Bittangabee Bay and Green Cape.

Popular with rock fisherman, Pulpit Rock sits neatly between Bittangabee Bay and Green Cape. The rock provides visitors with views of the stunning red rock cliffs and the ocean and coastline to the north. Access to Pulpit Rock is via a staircase off the service trail at Green Cape Rd approx. 4.6 km into the walk. While it is a small diversion off the destination trail, it is worthwhile to spend a few minutes and take in what will remain a highlight of the walk.

Ly-ee-moon Cemetery. A white stone and a lone white cross mark the graves of men, women and children tragically lost in the Ly-ee-moon shipwreck in 1886. The ship hit the reef during the night and while 16 lives were saved, a further 71 people were not. While some of the lost were not known by name, comments of remembrance are engraved on a nearby plaque. Located 300m north-west from Green Cape Lighthouse.

Mount Imlay Balawan Walking Track

A challenging undertaking pitting walkers against over 600m of elevation in just 3 km with steep trails and uneven footing, summiting rewards walkers with clear day coastline views spanning as far as Narooma to the north and across the state border to Mallacoota in the south. The reward of the views however pale as the locality is of indigenous spiritual and cultural significance, home to endangered, threatened and biogeographically significant botanical life and wildlife treasures.

Description: Rising out of the heavily forested Mount Imlay National Park and clearly visible by children in the school yards of Eden some 30 km away, Mount Imlay rises to 886m elevation and is the unchallenged high point of the Mount Imlay National Park. Known by local indigenous people as Balawan, the area holds great spiritual and cultural significance.

Closest Town: Eden 2550

Directions to the start: Follow Burrawang Rd into the Mt Imlay National Park. The walk starts at the Mount Imlay Carpark and Burrawang Picnic area.

Latitude and longitude: 37.18202°S, 149.75829°E

Grade: 5

Trail Quality: The track is narrow, steep and rough and with occasional uneven steps and under foot obstacles.

Time: 3 hours return

Distance: 6 km return

Amenities: None at the start, finish or along the way

Park Type: Mount Imlay National Park.

This walk delights flora enthusiasts with an array of colourful wildflowers and threatened and biogeographically significant plant species including the Mount Imlay Mallee, and the Mount Imlay Boronia. The former being discovered and named in 1980. There is a treasure trove of rare botanic species in the area which are thought to exist due to the unique environment emerging from an exposed outlook.

While the area is teaming with wildlife, many are nocturnal, and expectations during daylight should be around spotting Red-Necked Wallabies, majestic Glossy Black Cockatoos, and lyrebirds tilling the

undergrowth. If you are in the right place at the right time, you may spot some threatened species including the Tiger Quoll, koalas or the Long-Nosed Potaroo, and birdwatchers will feast upon the anticipation of sighting a Sooty Owl or an Olive Whistler.

From the Burrawang carpark, start your climb immediately. The track climbs steeply and is signposted and straight forward to follow. After spending time on the summit gazing up and down the coastline, walkers return to the Burrawang carpark the way they ascended.

Along the Way: The flora and fauna, endangered and threatened species as well as biogeographically unique species can be found.

Haycock Point to Barmouth Beach Walking Track

Taking in the rugged beauty and serenity of the Ben Boyd National Park, Haycock Point to Barmouth Beach walking track navigates windswept heath, thick woodlands and passes by rugged rock formations and dramatic cliffs with ocean views. The area is a refuge for wildlife and interesting birdlife which will be easily sighted along the way.

Description: Easily navigated and clearly marked, this relaxing coastal walk starts at the Haycock Picnic Area and makes its way through heath and wooded areas to Barmouth Beach. Views of the ocean, interactions with wildlife and the smells and sounds of nature make this walk both relaxing and stimulating. While it is a 2-hour return trip, consider packing a picnic and sitting on the rocks at Barmouth Beach for a mid-way recharge.

Along the Way:

If visiting the area during late winter to early spring, whales can be spotted migrating north.

Sitting just off the Haycock Point coastline, Haycock Rock marks the site of the shipwrecked Empire Gladstone which was enroute from Whyalla to Sydney carrying loads of steel car bodies.

Teaming with almost 150 species of birds in the vast Ben Boyd National Park, birdwatching along this route is a treat as the area is known to be a refuge for threatened species.

On approach to Barmouth Beach, Arched Rock Lookout is to the right and gives views of the unique Arched Rock – a natural structure that has been carved out by the ocean.

Closest Town: Eden, 2550

Start Location: Parking is at the Haycock Point Picnic Area at the end of Haycock Point Road.

Latitude and longitude: 36.9511029°S, 149.9358663°E

Grade: 3

Trail Quality: Gentle inclines, some obstacles underfoot however generally good walking.

Distance: 6 km return

Time: 2 hours

Amenities: Yes

Park Type: Haycock-Pambula Area – Ben Boyd National Park

Rocks at Barmouth Beach display their rich red qualities in deep contrast with the blue waters, the rocks at the river mouth appear red due to high iron content.

Broulee Island Nature Reserve Walk

There is plenty to enjoy about Broulee Island. Established as a nature reserve in 1972, Broulee Island covers 42 hectares, is steeped in history and teaming with birdlife and pristine rockpools.

Broulee island has a complex relationship with the mainland. In the 1800s Broulee Island was a bustling port and important stop for an increasing route of cargo ships to the south as road transport had not yet developed. By 1841 Broulee Island had an established population of 46 and various buildings including a court house, police station and Inn had been erected. Vessels of all sizes, including whaling boats were visiting daily to offload passengers and goods and restock for further trips. However, huge seas cut Broulee Island off from the mainland and the sandbar disappeared. The settlement was subsequently dismantled and moved upriver to Moruya where all the important shipping business was now administered. By 1859, the island was deserted.

Broulee Island offers walkers the serenity of a beach walk and the adventure of island exploration in one enjoyable walk. Connected to the mainland via tombolo and while it makes the island permanently accessible to walkers, the island is best visited at low tide to get the best access to the island and avoid making rock crossings between incoming waves on the ocean side of the island.

Closest Town: Broulee 2537

Start Location: Park at the Broulee Surf Club on Heath Street, Broulee.

Latitude and longitude: 35.8580000°S, 150.1764807°E

Grade: 3

Distance: 4 km loop

Time: 2 hours

Trail Quality: There is some scrambling over rocks and pebbly sections of beach, however most sections of the walk are relatively flat and easy to traverse.

Amenities: Yes

Park Type: Broulee Island Nature Reserve

Description: With an 'on again, off again' relationship with the mainland, Broulee Island is presently joined to the mainland via tombolo. Although there does not appear to be a clear record of

when the island has been joined to the mainland and when it has been independent, Broulee Island has been joined since at least the 1990s when it is believed the bitou bush weed arrived and fortified the sandbank.

Leaving the Broulee Beach Surf Lifesaving club – wander to the northern end of Broulee Beach and around the rocks to Shark Bay, cross the tombolo and the island is yours to explore. It is recommended to circumnavigate the island in a clockwise direction, keeping the ocean on your left.

The walk can be split into three sections. Starting on the northside, there are pristine rockpools to explore and some beautiful walking, this side of the island is often sheltered from the elements and great for a swim. As you come to the ocean side of the island there are more rockpools to explore and the exposed slanted beach is made up of small sized rocks. You are now in the more exposed part of the island and as you continue on to the southern side of the island any exposure elements on the day (wind/rain) are magnified. You will need to do a little rock hopping in the final leg of the walk before re-joining the tombolo.

Along the Way:

Roughly one third of the way through your journey around the island, you will encounter a large aboriginal midden and at low tide be sure to explore the rocks on the shorelines for fossilised shapes. There are many rock pools to inspect and plenty of places to sit and enjoy the ocean vista.

While there are some historical sites on the island, including Mrs Malabar's grave, sits in the bushland on the east side of the island. The advice is that the inner areas of the island are quite overgrown and snake encounters and ticks are not unusual if you choose to venture inland. The track to the gravesite is without signage.

Broulee Island, the first settlement in the Eurobodalla, was once the main town on the south coast. Up until it was dismantled in 1851, the island had been a bustling centre for passing vessels. Remains of the old drydock rail that once had purpose, and various footings remain and are mostly found on the north side of the island.

Scant remains of the once 17 to 20-metre-long jetty can be seen at Shellgrit Bay. The jetty was constructed in the 1920s and included light rail which was used to load shell grit from the bay onto ships for transport to Sydney. Shell grit was used in the building industry.

Gear: Sun protection, water, food and toilet paper. Swimmers are recommended as the water is very enticing on a hot day.

Montague Island Walking Track

Penguins, seals, solphins, whales, seabirds, a lighthouse, a boat ride and a tour guide ...

Montague Island, located just 9 km off the coastline of Narooma offers a unique walking experience. First sighted by Captain Cook in 1770, Montague Island, traditionally known as Barunguba has a rich history, amazing fauna and a lighthouse that has stood as guardian since 1881. Take in the beauty of the landscape while bearing witness to the conservation efforts in place to preserve the intriguing penguin population that calls Montague Island home.

This walk involves some pre planning and booking a boat ride from the mainland with an approved tour operator. Weather can be a determining factor on whether the tour goes ahead, and the best visiting months are during spring when the whales and fur seals are most active.

Closest Town: Narooma. Tours leave from Narooma wharf: Bluewater Drive, Narooma, and Bermagui wharf: Bermagui Harbour, Bermagui. Start walking from the Montague Island wharf.

Latitude and Longitude: 36.250528°S, 150.224467°E

Trail Quality: There is a jetty ladder that visitors need to be able to climb to get onto the island. The track is steep in places with steps. Stairs in the lighthouse. Guided Walk.

Tour Companies include:

Charter Fish Narooma, ph 0407 487702

Island Charters, ph 0408 428857

Lighthouse Charters, ph 0412 312478

Montague Island Game and Sport Fishing, ph 0447 951359

Narooma Charters & Montague Island Tours, ph 0407 909111

Be sure to check for the possibility of adding a lighthouse tour and whale watching to your trip.

Amenities: Yes

Grade: 3

Distance: 1.5 km

Time: 2 hours

Description: After making your way to Montague Island you will be guided around the islands Montague Island Walk to various sites of interest by an experienced and knowledgeable guide. The walk includes some steep steps as you climb up from the jetty and if you are lucky enough some more stairs as you ascend the lighthouse to get a glimpse into the life of a lighthouse keeper.

Although the walk is only 1.5 km in distance, there is some steep sections requiring average fitness. A tour guide will accompany your group around the points of interest on the island so no prior directions are needed.

Along the Way:

There are many aboriginal artifacts and middens on the island. The Yuin people have a strong connection with the island as it was used for ceremonies and as a men's teaching place by traditional owners.

Panoramic views out to sea and back to the coastline are vast and enticing. There is an abundance of sea life to observe, and the birdlife is varied.

The Penguin population on Montague Island is estimated at around 8000 at any given time.

Assumed to be a part of the mainland by Captain James Cook in 1770, the island, 'Montagu' was only named in 1790 after the master of the convict ship Surprise.

The island has been a welcomed piece of dry land for shipwrecked sailors.

During the gold rush, a seabird egg industry blossomed with eggs collected and sold to gold miners.

Hundreds of Fur seals make the island their home year-round and in spring, water from the blowholes of several whale species including the humpback whale and the southern right whale can be seen as they pass by while migrating south.

Shearwaters, a long-winged seabird, are thought to produce more than 12,000 chicks per year and the colonies on Montague Island appear to be increasing annually.

Montague
Island
Lighthouse

Montague Island

N
200 m

Lake Walking Track

Located in the central precinct of the Murramarang National Park, Lake Walking Track offers a flat formed walking track through natural bushland including the longest stand of spotted gum forests on the coastline and original coastal rainforest. Wildlife encounters are almost guaranteed and birdwatching opportunities are abundant.

Closest Town: Batemans Bay

Start Location: Parking is available on Lake Road, Durras North. Follow the signs via Mount Agony Road and North Durras Road.

Latitude and longitude: 35.63316°S, 150.29144°E

Trail Quality: Flat, formed pathway. Some obstacles and occasional steps. Limited signage.

Distance: 8 km return

Time: 3 hours

Amenities: Yes

Park Type: Murramarang National Park

Description: Following the northern shore of Durras Lake, the Lake Walking Track leads off the Durras Lake Discovery Trail. Signposted and on formed trail, this walk is easily followed and on a flat gradient. Wildlife encounters with eastern grey kangaroos, lyrebirds and wonga pigeons and are almost guaranteed. Goannas and wallabies may also be spotted.

Diverse flora including the coachwood and lilly pillies of the coastal rainforest, and the towering spotted gums forests give way to views of Durras Lake.

Along the Way:

Apart from the views of Durras Lake, this walk is a birdwatching heaven. Murramarang National Park boasts over 90 species of birdlife including a penguin colony, sea eagles, gannets, shearwaters, oystercatchers, peregrine falcons, several owl species, satin bowerbirds and more.

Depot Beach – Burrawang and Rainforest Walk

The Burrawang walking track and the Depot Beach Rainforest Walk are in the Depot Beach precinct of the Murramarang National Park. Enjoy the contrasting landscapes as you make your way along the Burrawang Walking track and onto the Depot Beach Rainforest Walk. Enjoy a coastal walk and a rainforest experience all at once. The Burrawang walking track travels on a journey across the Depot Beach headland taking in vast coastal views, coastal forests of spotted gums and plentiful bird watching opportunities. Walking through the Depot Beach Rainforest walk, with its towering green rainforest and lush undergrowth gives the atmosphere of an ancient and sacred location.

Closest Town: Batemans Bay

Start Location: Depot Beach Campground, off Depot Beach Rd, Depot Beach.

Latitude and longitude: 35.628651°S, 150.321445°E

Grade: 4

Trail Quality: Very steep, many steps, rough with obstacles underfoot. Clearly signposted.

Distance: 3.7 km

Time: 2 hours 30 minutes

Amenities: Yes, at the start and finish

Park Type: Murramarang National Park

Description: Starting at the Depot Beach campground, make your way to the fire station and turn right. At the top of the hill, the track head starts on your right. The trail is straight forward and signposted, it winds through the largest stand of spotted gum trees in coastal NSW. The headland gives ample opportunity to look out to sea and observe whales during migration season between May and November annually. After arriving at North Durras Beach, there is opportunity to enjoy the wild windswept views across the beach and back to the headland. Retrace your steps back to the Depot Beach campground for the rainforest portion of the walk.

From the Depot Beach Campground, walk 350m along Depot Beach Rd and turn right onto Depot Gutter Road, making your way to the Depot Beach Picnic Ground. From here the Depot Beach Rainforest Walk is clearly signposted and loops 400 metres back to where you started.

The rainforest in this area is listed as an endangered ecological community, and this is an enjoyable walk of a much gentler incline than the Burrawang Walking track. The track features all an ancient rainforest has to offer from the cool temperature and rich smells to the diverse flora and fauna. The trail includes steppingstones and logs that line the pathways and finishes back at Depot Beach with its white sands and inviting waters.

Along the Way:

There is an information centre at Depot Beach Campground and the staff are informative and friendly. It is worth stopping in for a chat before you walk.

The towering spotted gums along the Burrawang Track are the largest stand of their type along coastal NSW and sit in stark contrast to the dark green understory of the burrawangs. It is not uncommon to spot Lyrebirds busy in the undergrowth and swamp wallabies are commonly spotted darting through the bushland.

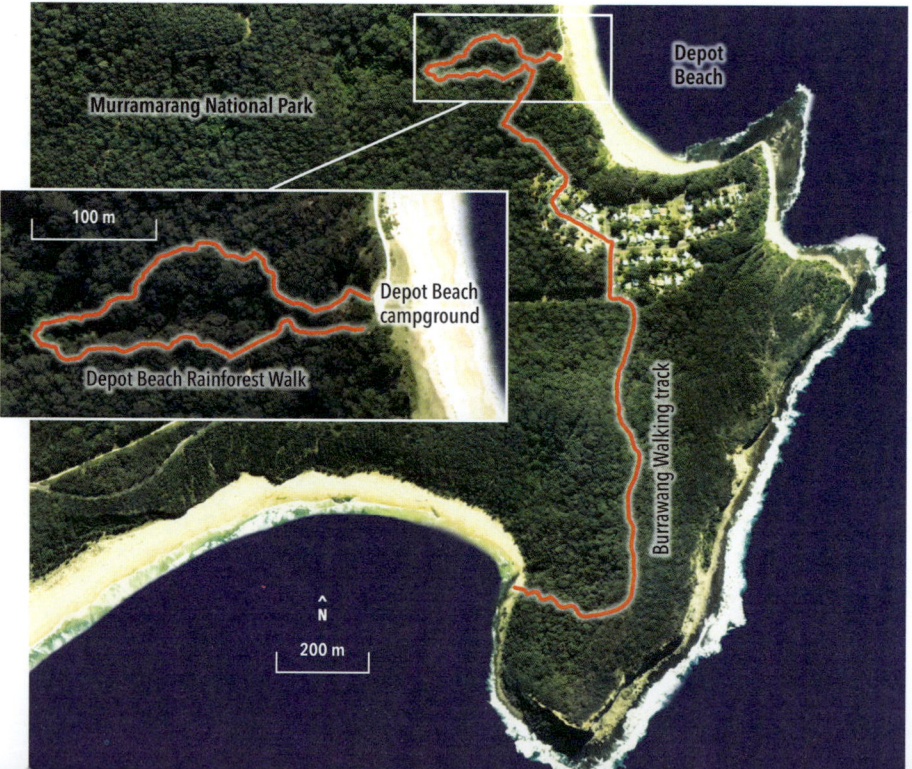

Mermaid Pool

While the walk is approximately 2 hours return, extra time should be allowed as the serenity of the location is bound to trump any evening plans you thought were important prior to arriving at the Mermaid Pool. This is a beach walk with a lagoon creek crossing at the start which will get your feet wet.

Description: From the Berrara Beach carpark make your way across the Berrara Creek Lagoon, and onto the soft white sands of South Berrara Beach. There is a family friendly lagoon here that is often populated with parents and their small people enjoying the outdoors. The creek crossing is best made at low tide and caution should be taken as the current is easily underestimated. It is not recommended in high tide or stormy conditions. Be sure to check the weather forecast and tidal information prior to leaving, as you need to cross the creek later upon return.

Closest Town: Berrara, 2540
Parking is available at the Berrara Beach carpark at 1 Berrara Road, Berrara.

Latitude and longitude:
35.208313°S, 150.547904°E

Grade: 3

Trail Quality: Steep in places, easy to follow. Ladders may be slippery in wet conditions. Limited signage. Water crossing cannot be avoided at the start and finish of this walk. The rest of the walk is straight forward along the beach, on soft or hard sand depending upon your preference.

Distance: 3 km return

Time: 2 hours

Amenities: Public Toilets at start/finish

Park Type: Conjola National Park

South Berrara Beach is a wide and expansive beach stretching to the south and to the destination, Mermaid Pool. The beach has light foot traffic and there is a remote feel to the area. Along the way there will be shells to inspect, and the ocean smell will ignite the senses. It is also likely you will shed your shoes and socks and enjoy the feel of the water as you make your way along.

The walk takes you south along South Berrara Beach for approximately 1.5 km where you will come to a rocky shelf. Make your way onto the rocks and the prize of the walk appears, the turquoise waters and the serenity make this a great place to enjoy a picnic and relax.

Uncrowded, it is likely you will have this special destination to yourselves.

Mermaid Pool is sheltered from the ocean on three sides by high rock walls, in high tide the ocean waves crash over the seaside rocks making a natural waterfall that replenishes the pool. There is plenty to explore in this area, the pool itself is the deepest rock pool in the Shoalhaven and has a sizable rock in the middle with a large overhang, there are plenty of sea snails, tiny fish and crabs to make your acquaintance. Sitting and basking in the sun with your feet in the water is also an option.

Along the Way:

Ocean views, shells and sea creatures along the water's edge.

400 m

Conjola National Park

Berrara Beach carpark

South Berrara Beach

Mermaid Pool

Pigeon House Mountain Didthul Walking Track

Located in the southern section of the Morton National Park and named by Captain James Cook in 1770 for its resemblance to a square dove house with a dome on top, Pigeon House Mountain and the Didthul walking track provide a diverse and captivating walking experience. The highlight of the walk is debatable; views from the summit spanning as far south as Bermagui and Jervis Bay, an adventurous scramble up ladders to the summit, the wildlife or rare flora, or just the spectacular views of the cliffs and gorges of the Budawang wilderness all competing for attention.

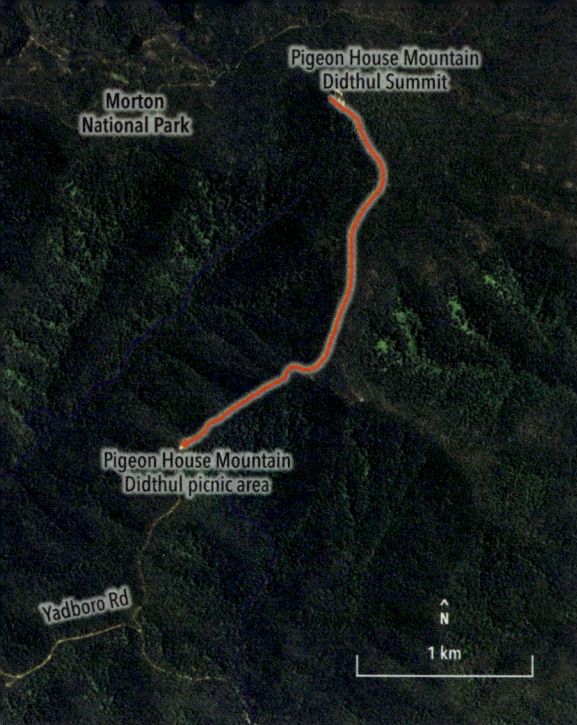

Park Type: Morton National Park

Closest Town: Milton 2538 and Ulladulla 2539

Start Location: Parking is available at the beginning of the Pigeon House Mountain Didthul walking track, next to Pigeon House Mountain Didthul picnic area off Yadboro Road.

Latitude and longitude: 35.3671450°S, 150.2554760°E

Grade: 4

Distance: 8 km return

Time: 3 hours

Amenities: Yes

Description: The most demanding section of the Pigeon House Mountain Didthul walking track is within the first 500m as walkers ascend a steep track and travel to the north east. Don't be deterred if you take a few breathers in the first kilometre, once you have crested the ridge the walk is much kinder. Easily navigated along the flat sandy pathway, walkers wind across the ridge and through open heath. From here the flora reflects the change in altitude as you first pass native species such as banksia and wattle, a short climb further and Yellow Stringybarks and Woolybutts appear and then the rare Pigeon House Ash as you approach the summit.

Constructed stairs become more frequent as you near the summit and the fabled steel ladders are the last steps prior to summiting.

Along the Way:

At the base of the peak there is a magnificent view over the Clyde River valley and peaks further field.

Narrawallee Inlet Walking Track

The Narrawallee Inlet Walking Track combines the pleasures of the Buckleys Point Walking Track, The Inlet Track and the Mangrove Track to provide a diverse walking experience. As the landscapes change, the habitat for both flora and fauna change, giving opportunity for many species to flourish in a relatively small area. While the sight of kangaroos grazing in the clearings and endless song of the local bird life is exhilarating, the highlight of the walk is the inlet at Narrawallee Creek and its natural and untouched beauty.

Directions: Leaving Narrawallee Creek Road, walk in a southern direction along Buckleys Point Trail. The trail tracks through the Narrawallee Creek Nature Reserve, passing a junction with the Mangrove Trail. Ignore this

Closest Town: Lake Conjola

Start Location: Park at the track head of Buckleys Point Trail on the corner of Narrawallee Creek Road and Buckleys Point Trail, Conjola Park.

Latitude and longitude: 35.278682°S, 150.463916°E

Grade: 3

Trail Quality: Rough under foot at times, some inclines, signposted.

Distance: 7.7 km

Time: 3.5 hours

Park Type: Narrawallee Creek Nature Reserve

trail – you'll come back to it later. Keep heading towards the coast, until you arrive at a junction with the Inlet Trail which is on your right. Take the Inlet Trail and head south. When you reach the junction of the Mangrove Trail, continue south along the Inlet Trail to Narrawallee Inlet. After taking in the beauty of the inlet, retrace your steps to the junction with the Mangrove Trail on your left. Turn left and follow the Mangrove Trail as it tracks west hugging Narrawallee Creek and eventually deviating to the north to link back with the Buckleys Point Trail. Turn left onto the Buckleys Point Trail and return to junction with Narrawallee Creek Road.

Along the Way:

The Narrawallee Creek Nature Reserve is the traditional land of the Wanda Wandian people. With an abundance of waterways, creeks, lagoons and the ocean, the area was a haven for important food gathering.

In cooler months whales are seen migrating and the beaches provide a great vantage point for the area's playful dolphin population.

This walk takes you through diverse landscapes of lagoon, swamps and woodlands, each playing host to an abundance of diverse flora and fauna.

While the beaches in the reserve are important nesting grounds for the endangered pied oystercatcher and the critically endangered hooded plover, the swamp forest, lush with swamp mahogany, provides food source for the swift parrot, yellow-bellied glider and regent honeyeater amongst more rare and endangered birdlife.

Minnamurra River to Kiama Blowhole

The first leg of the Kiama Coastal Walking Track, this is a spectacular coastal walk with some unique natural masterpieces to appreciate along the way. Anticipation is high from the start, with the views from the Minnamurra Whale Watching Platform stretching north across the beautiful Minnamurra River mouth and south toward Jones Beach. If you are there in the right season, Whale sightings are almost guaranteed. The beautiful and intriguing Cathedral Rocks and Bombo Headland combined with the special effects of the Kiama Blowhole make this an exciting part of the Kiama Coastal Walking Track.

Description: Starting at James Oates reserve, enjoy the vast open space at the mouth of the Minnamurra River before making your way along the grass path close to the water's edge. Head south east towards Minnamurra Headland and the Minnamurra Whale watching platform. From here trend toward and past Jones Beach, coming to Cathedral Rocks, one of nature's masterpieces. After viewing Cathedral Rocks, follow the track up and along Cliff Drive past Cameron Boyd Reserve and the beautiful Boneyard Beach. Continue along the pathway onto Bombo Headland.

Bombo Headland features basalt columns jutting out of the landscape like something from a space scene. A combination of the colours and column shapes of the rocks makes for a unique landscape which is often photographed and used in film making. The rock formations accumulated

in their current shape in response to both environmental exposure and quarrying and mining efforts in the area between 1880 and the early 1900s. After spending some time taking in Bombo Headland, Bombo Beach lies below and is a 1.2 kilometre long predominantly surf beach. The walk continues along the sand of Bombo Beach and climb the steps at the southern end making its way left along Gipps Street and over the headland passing Black Beach Rock Pool and into Kiama Harbour.

Make your way south along Black Beach foreshore and onto the headland. As you circle the headland you come to the Kiama Blowhole Lookout. The blowhole is spectacular, and the smell of the ocean is sublime. There are a few more points of interest before leaving the headland including George Bass Lookout and the Kiama Lighthouse. Continue along the pathway and join Blowhole Point Road to make your way back down into Kiama township and the finish of the walk.

Along the Way:

Whale Watching: Enjoy the views of migrating whales from the Minnamurra headland on the purpose-built elevated platform. Between late May and July, migrating Humpback Whales are frequently spotted on their journey north to warmer waters. The Whales move south again between September and November accompanied by their calves.

There are various Cafes and restaurants to finish your walk at on the Kiama foreshore. Kiama train station is located on Railway parade Kiama and travels to Minnamurra station for the return trip.

Closest Town: Kiama

Start Location: James Oates reserve, Charles Avenue, Minnamurra. Access the track head near the boat ramp.

Latitude and longitude:
34.628836°S, 150.857826°E

Grade: 3

Trail Quality: Mostly paved, some sand walking, some rocky sections, some steps. Clearly signposted.

Distance: 8.4 km

Time: 4 hours

Amenities: Yes, at the start and several along the way

Park Type: Urban

Bomaderry Loop Track

Following the picturesque Bomaderry creek along both the Bomaderry Creek Eastern Walk, crossing the weir and returning via the Bomaderry Creek Western Walk. The landscape is diverse and interesting, within minutes of staring you enter a world of enormous boulders, rock overhangs and rainforest foliage. The gorge walls at times rise dramatically skyward and all the while the creek flows calmly through and around the rocks on the creek bed.

Description: Starting from Bomaderry Creek Picnic Area, make your way south along the track behind the amenities, taking the Bomaderry Creek Eastern Walk. This walk follows Bomaderry Creek with the water on your right. From here the dramatic boulders become normal landscape features and there is soon a bench to take a seen and ponder your surrounds.

Continue along the trail, and at the bridge crossing on your right, continue straight, again keeping the creek on your right. There is a creek crossing at the ford and not long after you cross back again and continue around the outer bend of the creek. Cross the next bridge and continue down the stairs to the series of fords. Another 400 metres on and you reach the intersection with the Bomaderry Creek Western Walk.

Closest Town: Bomaderry

Start Location: Bomaderry Creek Picnic Area, Narang Rd, Bomaderry.

Latitude and longitude: 34.8452583°S, 150.5914243°E

Grade: 3

Trail Quality: Rough track, easily followed, stairs and obstacles along the way. Signposted.

Distance: 4 km

Time: 3 hours

Amenities: Yes

Park Type: Bomaderry Creek Regional Park

As you continue there are views overlooking the gorge. There is a tangle of fords and a bridge to navigate before finally crossing over the creek and continuing back along the creek with the water on your right again.

The trail winds along beside the creek, at times close to the water and at times in a close by nature track. The next set of steps comes with just 800 metres remaining in the walk. Continue and cross the longest bridge on the walk, navigate some fords and make your way up some steps until you come to the fork in the track. Stay left and make your way up to the picnic area and the end of the walk.

Along the Way:

Keep an eye on the rocks and cliff faces as you pass by, there is evidence the gorge was important in aboriginal times, with axe grinding grooves and rock shelters visible. A combination of the abundant water source, the fish stock and the shade and shelters in the area made it a hospitable environment for Aboriginal people.

Wildflowers, Wildflowers, Wildflowers. Bomaderry Creek Nature Reserve puts on a special wildflower display with Guinea Flower, the vulnerable Albatross Mallee and Bauer's Midge Orchid all showing off during spring. Growing nowhere else in the world, the endangered Bomaderry Zieria, adds to the magical landscapes of the park.

In 1938, a weir was built on Bomaderry Creek for the purpose of providing water to the township of Bomaderry. The weir, has been partially dismantled and fish, including Australian Bass make their way freely along the creek.

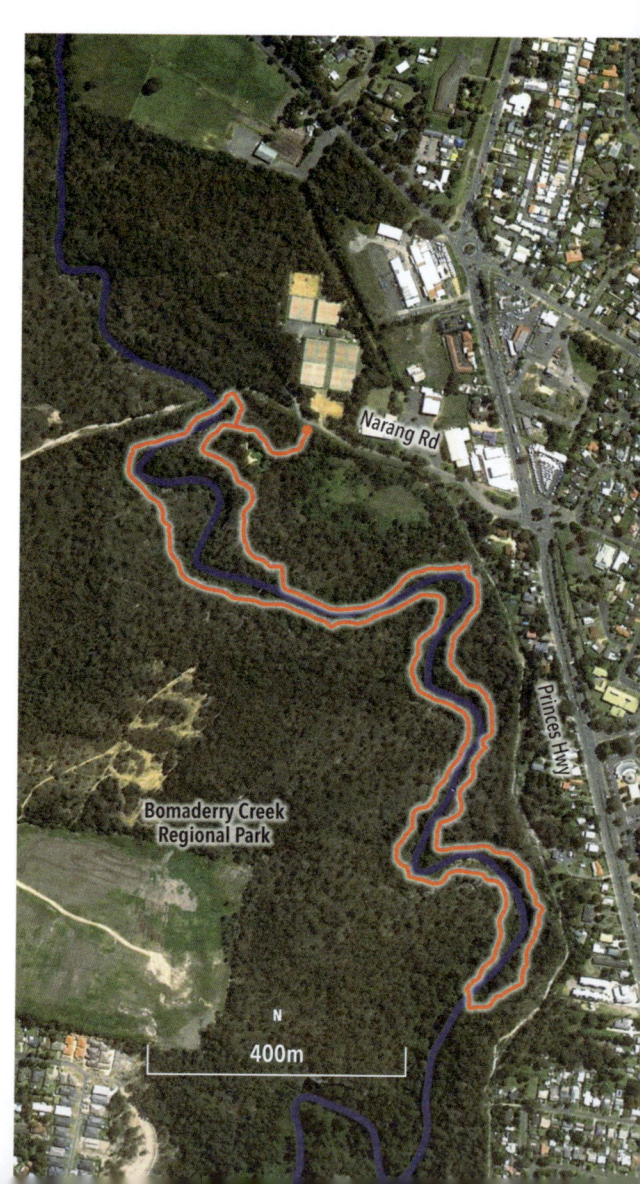

Mount Keira, Byarong Park to Robertson Lookout

A picturesque walk on part of the popular Mount Keira Ring Track to an excellent lookout. This walk trends upwards through stands of rainforest with filtered views until you reach Robertson Lookout. Make your way onto the viewing platform where the views of Mount Keira and the Illawarra coastline present a contrasting and magnificent picture.

Description: Starting in Byarong Park, make your way to the far end, parallel with Mount Keira Road. The track head is on the edge of the bushland behind the information board in a small stand of trees.

The sign at the start of the track indicates 'Mt Keira Ring Track'. Enter the bushland here and make your way along the single trail, some boardwalk and bush steps to a road crossing at the gates of the girl guide camp, only 150m after you start. Dogleg right then left, following the signs. Make your way along the gradual bush steps up the hillside. After 200 metres you will come to an intersection, turn left, and continue toward 'The Jumpers'.

Continue along the trail as it climbs gently in parallel with Mount Keira

Closest Town: Mount Keira

Start Location: Byarong Park, Mount Keira Road, Mount Keira.

Latitude and longitude: 34.407714°S, 150.848955°E

Grade: 4

Trail Quality: Short steep hills, many steps, formed trail with some obstacles under foot. Clearly signposted.

Distance: 6.3 km

Time: 3 hours 30 minutes

Amenities: Yes

Park Type: Illawarra Escarpment State Conservation Area

Road. The vegetation is consistent with lush forest, thick undergrowth and striking greenery including tall tree ferns. As you leave the canopy of trees you come out of the forested area beside Camp Road. The signs indicate where to re-enter the bushland on the left and continue. The track winds through stands of fan palms and makes its way up to Camp Road, crossing over and continuing along, now parallel with Mount Keira Road.

As you come to the steel steps leading up to the right (these continue along the Mt Keira Ring Track), pass by the left of the steps and continue as signposted along Robertsons Lookout track and at the next sign, turn left and continue. The stone bush steps take over and you eventually climb up some steel steps to a high point and some filtered views across the bushland. At the small opening in the bushland there is an option to the right, ignore it and continue straight ahead, heading back into the bushland.

The trees in this next section form a tunnel effect and the walking is pleasant with lots of leaf litter under foot. After some gentle downhill, the track climbs again and continues to a clearing with picnic tables. Continue to the left and to on to Robertsons Lookout and viewing platform.

Retrace your steps to return to Byarong Park to finish.

Along the Way:

Robertson Lookout offers commanding views across Mt Keira and the Illawarra coastline. Mount Keira looms over the Illawarra at 464 metres above sea level and is an iconic landmark in the area.

Mount Keira is sacred ground of the Wodi Wodi people. From the Dharawal language group, 'Keira', derives from the words Geera and Djera – Wodi Wodi words for the mountain.

West Rim Track

A walk around the West Rim Track at Fitzroy Falls delights with a tour of eight lookouts all featuring sublime views into the stunning Yarrunga Valley. This lush rainforest and tall eucalypt forested area hosts dramatic views across to the picturesque and wild Fitzroy Falls. Visiting 8 lookouts, the experience of the falls differs at every lookout, from viewing up close limited sections of the falls to vast sweeping views taking in the entire valley. There is a myriad of perspectives of the 80 metre falls as the waters make their way into the valley below. Birdlife in the area is plentiful and taking binoculars on this walk is recommended.

Description: The track is clearly signposted. Starting at the Fitzroy Falls information Centre, take the underpass underneath Nowra Road and the first lookout comes up quickly, only 150 metres after starting. The main viewpoint of the area, you are close to the top of the Falls. Continue along the track to Jersey Lookout which gives a more front on view, again of the upper falls.

After Jersey Lookout, you will encounter Richardson Lookout, Twin Falls Lookout, Paine's Lookout, The Grotto and Starkey's Lookout. Continue along the trail which tracks in the shape of a long curve around to the final lookout, Renown Lookout. Renown Lookout sits at some distance from and positioned straight on to the waters of Fitzroy Falls as they tumble to the valley below. Once you reach Renown Lookout, retrace your steps to finish the walk back at the Fitzroy Falls Information centre.

Closest Town: Fitzroy Falls 2577

Start Location: Fitzroy Falls Information Centre, 1301 Nowra Rd, Fitzroy Falls.

Latitude and longitude: 34.646793°S, 150.482674°E

Grade: 3

Trail Quality: Formed Track, some obstacles, many steps. Clearly signposted.

Distance: 3.5 km

Time: 2 hours

Amenities: Yes, at the start

Park Type: Morton National Park

Along the Way:

Wildflowers in the area are a delight

during spring and summer with the purple flowering chocolate lilies a highlight.

The diverse landscape of Morton National Park includes rain forested areas highlighted by a variety of ferns, moss and tall eucalyptus forests featuring a variety of Sydney peppermint, spotted gum and rare pigeon house ash to name a few.

Consistent with a diverse landscape comes a diverse birdlife and the Fitzroy Falls area is teaming with an array of birdlife. Green Catbirds, lyrebirds, Satin Bowerbirds, ground parrots, eagles and falcons. The calls of the birdlife in the area give life to the precious surrounds.

Fitzroy Falls Visitor Centre

Nowra Rd

Twin Falls Lookout

The Grotto

Paines Lookout

Jersey Lookout

Richardson Lookout

Starkeys Lookout

Morton National Park

N

300 m

Renown Lookout

East Rim and Wildflower Walk

Spotted with five lookouts, all with varying views and specialties, the East Rim and Wildflower Walk takes you on a journey of both discovery and immersion. Locally the Fitzroy Falls views are stunning. As you make your way along the lookouts the rugged Morton National Park comes into view with the range toward Bundanoon, Yarrunga Creek Gorge. Mount Moollattoo and Mount Carrialoo all featuring along this walk.

Description: Starting at the Fitzroy Falls Information Centre, the Wildflower Walking Track journeys to the May Lookout and on to the Warrawong Lookout. From the Warrawong Lookout the East Rim Track takes over and the journey continues to Lamond Lookout. From Lamond Lookout, Valley View Lookout is the last lookout before reaching Yarrunga Lookout and the turnaround point. Retrace your steps back to the information centre to finish.

Along the Way:

As you reach May Lookout, keep an eye out for the large termite mound.

This area is known for Lyrebird activity, and they can often be heard busy at work in the undergrowth.

The Warrawong Lookout provides striking views of Fitzroy Falls and the surrounding sandstone cliff faces. Views in the opposite direction extend down the Yarrunga Valley. Warrawong Lookout marks the end of the Wildflower Walk and the start of the East Rim Walk.

Lamond Lookout looks south to Mount Carrialoo plateau which stands at 687 metres above sea level. Lamond also offers views across to the Renown Lookout at the furthest point of the West Rim Track.

Valley View looks down across the treetops into the valley, and with the large sandstone cliffs it feels like a Blue Mountains vista.

Yarrunga Lookout enjoys the vast vistas of the tall eucalypt forests and rainforests below. The escarpments come to life at this lookout, it is the most southern point on the walk.

Helpful Plaques provide information in identifying flora in the area throughout the walk.

Closest Town: Fitzroy Falls

Start Location: Fitzroy Falls Information Centre, 1301 Nowra Rd, Fitzroy Falls.

Latitude and longitude: 34.646793°S, 150.482674°E

Grade: 3

Trail Quality: Many Steps, formed track, some obstacles. Clearly Signposted.

Distance: 6.7 km

Time: 3 hours

Amenities: Yes, at the start

Park Type: Morton National Park

Kangaroo River Walking Track

Sometimes it is great to keep things simple. This is a straightforward walk along an uncomplicated and natural bush track to the water's edge at Lake Yarrunga. The walk is unpretentious and rewards with an uncrowded waterside location to relax and enjoy. The river's edge offers a relaxing place to picnic or do some fishing and it's a popular place for swimming.

Description: This fire trail walk is all about the destination. Leaving the roadside carpark, make your way around the gate and down the at times steep Kangaroo River Track. This track is wide and easy to navigate. Stay on the main trail all the way down to the edge of the beautiful waters of Lake Yarrunga, on the Kangaroo River. Retrace your steps to return to the carpark.

Along the Way:

The area is a birdwatchers paradise and includes gang gangs, cockatoos, lorikeets and an array of waterbirds once you reach the lake.

Bass and Carp are often fished from the waters of Lake Yarrunga, if you are keen on fishing this may be a good spot. There is ample room for several groups to swim, fish and picnic.

Closest Town: Kangaroo Valley

Start Location: Intersection of Tallowa Dam Road and Kangaroo River Firetrail, Moolattoo, 15 km west of Kangaroo Valley. Tallowa Dam Road is called Mount Skanzi Road in Kangaroo Valley.

Latitude and longitude: 34.772378°S, 150.384356°E

Grade: 4

Trail Quality: Very steep, clear path, some obstacles. Limited signage.

Distance: 7 km

Time: 3 hours

Amenities: No

Park Type: Morton National Park

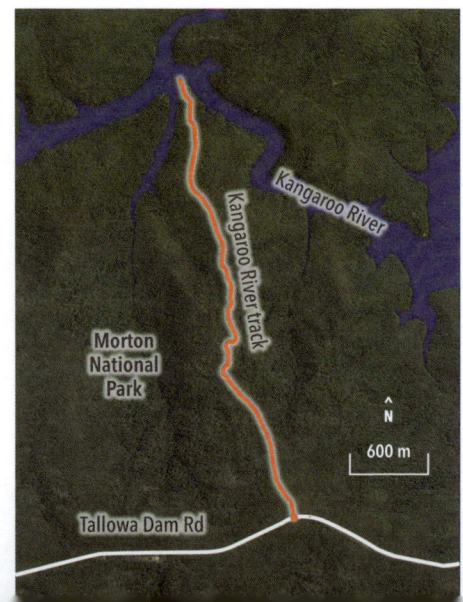

Missingham Lookout Track Walk

With commanding views over Kangaroo Valley and the picturesque Carrington Falls Gorge, this walk highlights the beauty of Budderoo National Park from a high vantage point. Flora and Fauna in the area are bountiful and this is one of the easiest walks with great rewards.

Description: Leaving Nellies Glen Picnic area, start along the Missingham Lookout Track. The Kangaroo Valley Gorge is to your left. Pass the gate and after a few minutes you will come to an intersection. Turn right and continue along the Missingham Lookout Track. There are two trails with almost identical names here – **be careful to keep to Missingham Lookout Track and don't turn left onto the Missingham Lookout Trail**!

The next intersection is at the intersection of the Missingham Lookout Track and the Nellies Glen Loop Track. Take the left option, staying on the Missingham Lookout Track. Continue along the trail crossing the ford and at the next intersection turn left, still on the Missingham Lookout Track. Stay on this trail and at the next intersection veer right. The next intersection is at the Missingham Lookout Track and the Missingham Steps, continue left down Missingham Lookout Track. At the end of the track, a further 10 metres on is Missingham West Lookout.

On the return leg, after the intersection of the Missingham Lookout Track and Missingham Steps, continue straight and take the side trip down to Missingham East Lookout.

To return, retrace your steps back to Nellies Glen picnic area.

Closest Town: Robertson

Start Location: Nellies Glen Picnic Area, Nellies Glen Trail, Robertson. 1.8 km south of the intersection of Cloonty Road and Jamberoo Mountain Road, Robertson.

Latitude and longitude: 34.623049°S, 150.656334°E

Grade: 3

Trail Quality: Formed Track, limited obstacles. Signposted.

Distance: 4 km

Time: 2 hours

Amenities: Yes, at the start

Park Type: Budderoo National Park

Along the Way:

Birdlife in the area is plentiful – the park is home to the superb fairy wren, bowerbirds, lyrebirds, Yellow-Tailed Black Cockatoo and the vibrant King Parrot. Missingham West and Missingham East Lookouts are both great places to look for eagles and flacons riding the thermals from the gorge below.

A short drive away is the Minnamurra Rainforest Centre, located at Minnamurra Falls Road, Jamberoo, the centre is a hub of information about Budderoo National Park and gateway to some more beautiful walks including the Minnamurra Falls Walk.

Tahmoor Gorge Loop Track

A natural walk through the rugged and beautiful Tahmoor Gorge. This walk is maintained by locals and recommended for walkers with experience. Taking you past amazing waterholes including See through Pools, Mermaid Pools and Olympic Pools. Lots of lookouts, great views and a close-up experience with Morton National Park.

Description: From the makeshift carpark, the trail passes beneath the Rockford Rd bridge and tracks downstream, following the river's edge on what is known locally as the Matilda Track. After roughly a kilometre, the track leaves the river's edge and climbs above the riverbank and continues. The first stop is See Through Pools which is accessed via a split in the trail to the left at approximately 1.1 km. You will also find loose directions marked on the rocks in paint with 'ST' leading the way to these pools.

Return to the main track and continue. The next diversion is to the majestically stunning Mermaid Pools. While picturesque, and a place to sit and gaze upon, it is not recommended to swim here. Water from the Bargo River gushes over the rocks into the deep waterhole below making for quite a spectacle but once in the water, swimmers find there is no viable way out of the hole without climbing a rope. Serious injuries have occurred here.

Retrace your steps to the junction and turn left along Matilda's Track. The next point of interest is Mermaids Lookdown, with views worthy of a postcard. From here it is a short walk to the logbook perched in a red box and mounted on some stakes. The logbook also includes a handy map that you can photograph to use as you

Closest Town: Tahmoor

Start Location: Mermaids Pool and Tahmoor Gorge carpark, Charlies Point Road, Bargo. Just south of the Rockford Road intersection.

Latitude and longitude: 34.250919°S, 150.606498°E

Grade: 5

Trail Quality: Steep, steps, rock hopping, at times unformed. Steep areas have chains and ropes attached to assist if needed. Informally signposted and marked.

Distance: 10 km

Time: 3 hours 45 minutes

Amenities: No

Park Type: Morton National Park

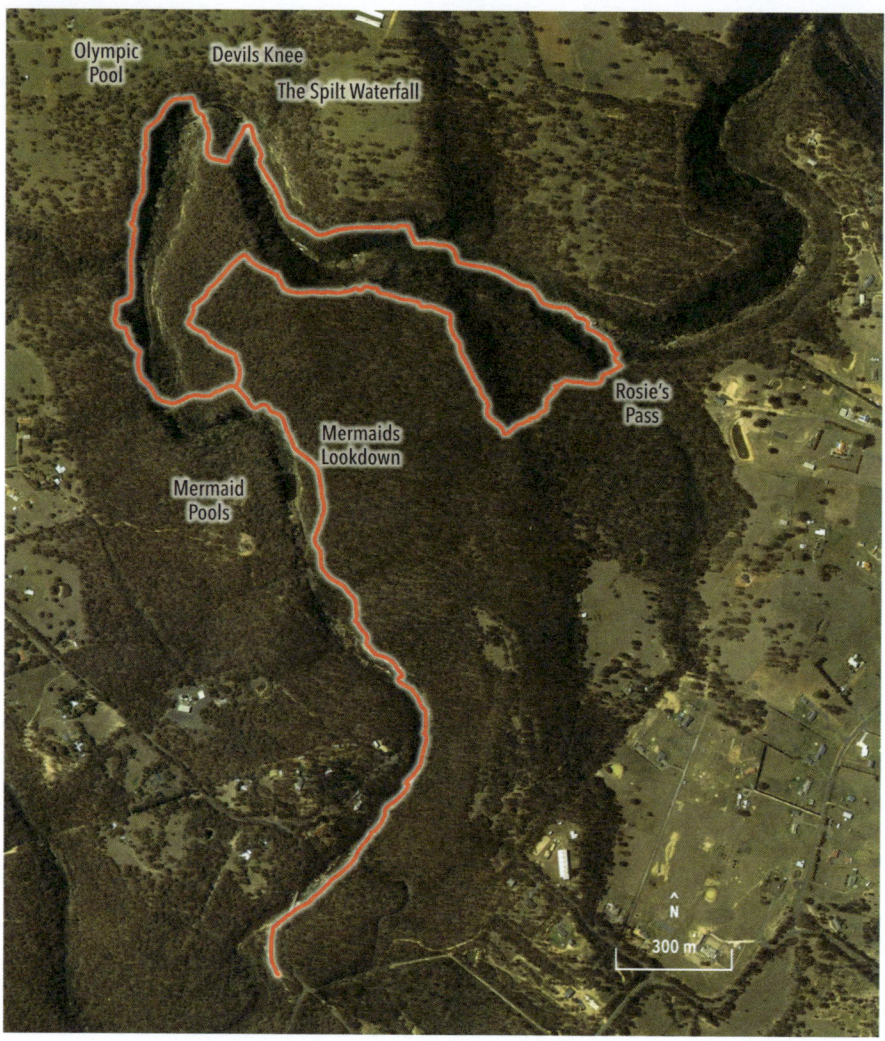

Olympic Pool · Devils Knee · The Spilt Waterfall · Rosie's Pass · Mermaids Lookdown · Mermaid Pools · N · 300 m

travel along. At the junction, turn left and follow Jacks Pass steeply down into the gorge. The trail from here is a mix of trail and rock platforms, there are several small bridge crossings and soon you reach Olympic Pool on the bend of the river. Not long after Olympic Pool and Devils Knee, pass by the Spilt Waterfall and cross to the out bank of the river before crossing back a few hundred metres further downstream.

As you reach Rosie's Pass, the track leaves the flowing river and heads steeply uphill away from the water. Looping back around along the trail which sits much higher now, there are several lookouts along the way before

arriving back at the red box. From this junction turn left returning past Mermaid Pools turnoff and See Through Pools turnoff, both now on your right and making your way back to the finish under Rockford Bridge.

Along the Way:

The map at the logbook details the discovery of the way through Tahmoor Gorge by Jo Hafey and Robert Sloss and the formation and upkeep of the gorge tracks which has been continued throughout the years by Robert Sloss and Rosie.

See Through Pools is a great place to swim and lives up to its name. At times you will spot carp scouring the bottom of the waterfall for anything to feed on.

The Green Track

Enjoy the gentle walking experience of The Green Track around Bungonia National Park. Passing through open woodlands, this walk has many short side trips to the best viewing points along the way. Get a glimpse of the rugged and unforgiving limestone cliffs of Bungonia Slot Canyon from above, the beautiful Jerrara Falls or the intriguing Mass Cave. If wildlife is your thing, Wallabies, Kangaroos, and Goannas are ever present and wildflowers throughout spring are spectacular.

Description: The trail is marked all the way around with green markers and arrows. At times there will be red markers as well – this is where different walks share a section of trail. There are several picnic areas to visit and side trips that will lengthen your walk if you take them.

From the De Kerrilleau picnic area, the track starts on single track through open wooded area. Much of this walk is through similar terrain on undulating ground. At times the forest thickens but for the most part you can see right through the trees for some distance.

Closest Town: Goulburn

Start Location: De Kerrilleau picnic area. Bungonia Lookdown Road near Adams Lookout Road, Bungonia.

Latitude and longitude: 34.806144°S, 150.012600°E

Grade: 3

Trail Quality: Mostly an easy walk, some rough sections, track is either single track or service road and well signposted. Some side tracks are a little less kept.

Distance: 6.7 km

Time: 3 hours

Amenities: Yes, at the start

Park Type: Bungonia National Park

The first stop along the way is at the David Reid Picnic Area. (**Side Trip: Molly O'Neill Nature Walk**). Pass by the amenities block and onward to the top of the parking lot and veer left, following the Green hiker direction sign and pass the locked gate. After some undulating trail you come to an intersection with a sign to Mass Cave. (**Side Trip: Mass Cave**). Turn Left, the trail in the next section is a little rough however it evens out shortly. Cross the small bridge over the dry gully and continue to the next picnic area. (**Side Trip: Adams Lookout**).

In the picnic area, follow the green direction signs past the locked gate and on towards Jerrara Lookout. The track forks with the Jerrara Lookout option on your right and the track continuing your left. (**Side trip: Jerrara Lookout**).

Continue along the Green Track, there are more directional markers at just the right time. The track passes two informal trails off to the right, both trails have an unfenced lookout over the gorge below and into the distance. Arriving at Bungonia Campground, take the Green Track as signed and continue crossing the Lookdown Track as you come into De Kerrilleau Picnic Ground to finish.

Along the Way – Side Trips:

Molly O'Neill Nature Walk – Approximately 600 metres return. Molly O'Neill was a passionate amateur botanist who was dedicated to exploring and documenting the botany of the Bungonia National Park. There are information signs along the way identifying some of the flora of the wildflower plentiful area. Fauna is also plentiful with Wallabies, Kangaroos and Goanna sightings common. This track takes you out to the Bungonia Lookdown.

Bungonia Lookdown – About 50 metres from the Molly O'Neill Track

Taking in views across the Ettrema Wilderness area in Morton National park, the lookdown sits above Bungonia Slot Canyon and has views deep into the rugged and wild limestone outcrops of the Bungonia Creek Gorge.

Mass Cave – Turn right at the intersection (it's signed), it's an 80 metre side trip.

In the 1950s this cave was used for church services. The cave goes into the hill some way and a headlamp is required for anything further than a cursory look. The formations in the cave are spectacular. There is a gate at the opening to Mass Cave which is at times locked. Check at the office if you are planning of entering the cave.

Adams Lookout – An easy 400 metre return walk.

The only lookout to have views into Bungonia Slot Canyon, this is a great place for viewing the limestones canyon below or looking across to Frome Hill. The platform at Adams Lookout has several viewing levels and if you look sky ward you may see a resident pair of Peregrine Falcons surfing the thermals.

Jerrara Lookout – 80 metres return.

Not to be confused with Jerrara Canyon Lookout, this very short detour is the right hand side option at the fork in the trail. You will come to a small fenced rock ledge with views across to Jerrara Falls. The more rain there has been the more spectacular the falls are.

Bungonia National Park

Jerrara
Lookout

Adams Lookout •

• Mass Cave

• Bungonia Lookdown

Molly O'Neill Nature Walk

Bungonia Lookdown Rd

De Kerrilleau
picnic
area

N

400 m

Southern

The Big Hole Walking Track

An adventurous walk culminating in a visit to The Big Hole, a 100-metre deep and 50-metre-wide chasm in the earth. With a river crossing to navigate, this walk has a sense of fun about it as you are on your way to The Big Hole. It is hard to get your head around The Big Hole and after viewing it, it remains just as mysterious.

Description: The walk starts at the Berlang Campground and there is signage at the track head. Follow the track to the Shoalhaven River. Here you need to ford through the river, as there is no bridge. The river crossing can vary from a rock hopping experience to wading depending upon the rainfall in the previous weeks. The trail winds its way gently uphill and then evens out before coming to The Big Hole.

There is a viewing platform, and it is just as well. There are no real warnings that you are about to come across a monstrous hole in the earth! After spending some time wondering, how, when and by whom... return via the same route to the Berlang Campground.

Closest Town: Braidwood.

Start Location: Berlang Campground, Deua National Park. From Braidwood, drive south for 30 minutes along the Cooma Road. Turn left at the sign to 'Berlang/The Big Hole'. The Berlang campground is another 700 metres on.

Latitude and longitude: 35.724766°S, 149.646330°E

Grade: 4

Trail Quality: Formed track, some obstacles, many steps. The signage is limited on this walk.

Distance: 4 km

Time: 2 hours

Amenities: Yes

Park Type: Deua National Park

Along the Way:

Thought to be approximately 400 million years in the making, the Big Hole is a limestone marvel which was traversed by an adventurous soul in 1862. Armed with just a candle to explore the bottom, the young man used saproling timber and rope to descend and ascend the intriguing roofless cave.

The views are as you walk along the trail are at their most panoramic on the return trip.

Rumour is, a resident Lyrebird makes its way out of the Big Hole daily to rummage for supplies.

The Big Hole track

Berlang
Campground

Berlang Rd

Cooma Rd

Shoalhaven River

Deua National Park

N

200 m

Mount Coree Summit Walking Track

A road walk to the summit of the northernmost peak of the Australian Alps. Mount Coree has panoramic views across the Namadgi and Brindabella National Parks. While it is recommended to do this walk outside of snow season, if you are well prepared and experienced in snow events, this walk can be a beautiful experience under light snow conditions.

Description: Best visited between late October and mid-March to avoid random snowfalls, there are signs along the road indicating the feasibility of driving into the Brindabella National Park on any given day.

Leaving the Coree Campground, the walk makes its way downwards and over a bridge crossing the headwaters of Coree Creek, before starting the climb toward the summit. The trail is management track which is a shared road and at times there could be mountain bikers or vehicles pass by.

As you ascend further into the route, the track gets progressively rougher. The route is easily followed and there is a creek crossing that fluctuates in water level depending upon recent rainfall.

The summit reveals vast and impressive views of Brindabella National Park and the Namadgi National Park. While Mount Coree summit is one of the only mountain walks in this book that you can drive to the summit, you need a 4WD and even then the gates may be closed.

Retrace your steps back down to the Coree Campground to finish.

Closest Town: Canberra

Start Location: Coree Campground. On Coree Summit Road, Uriarra, just off Two Sticks Road.

Latitude and longitude: 35.297257°S, 148.807707°E

Grade: 3

Trail Quality: Smooth road ascending upwards. Not signposted.

Distance: 5.6 km

Time: 2 hours 30 minutes

Amenities: Yes

Park Type: Brindabella National Park

Along the Way:

Mount Coree, is the northern most peak of the Australian Alps and stand at 1421 metres above sea level. The Coree Trigonometry

Station sits on the summit of Mount Coree and was used for survey purposes in the area.

Coree Mountain was a known hunting ground for moths by Indigenous Australians. Coree is the aboriginal name for moth and the Bogong Moth was plentiful in the area.

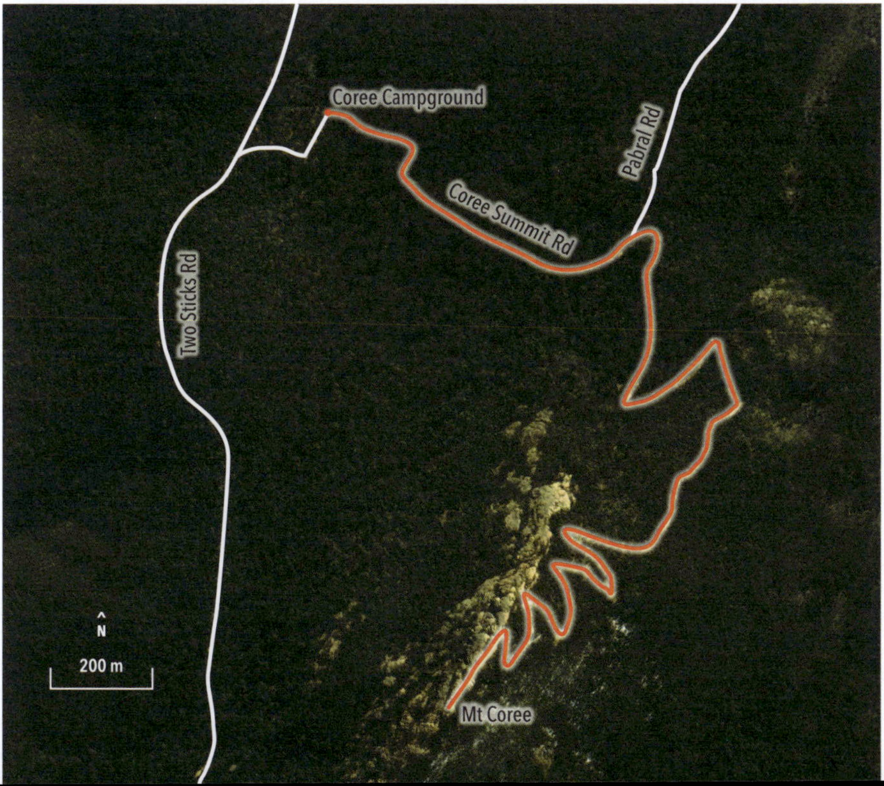

South Glory Cave and Yarrangobilly River Walk

Nestled away in the Kosciuszko National Park is the Yarrangobilly area, an area brimming with natural wonders. Limestone caves are the highlight of the walk with stalagmites, stalactites, shawls and cave coral to intrigue and explore. The limestone, Glory Arch won't disappoint either. Returning via the spring fed thermal pool and with a short climb to the end, this is a rewarding walk.

Description: Make your way first to Yarrangobilly Visitor Centre. To enter the caves requires a cave ticket which can be purchased here. Maps are also available from the Visitors Centre. Drive or walk back to the Glory Cave Carpark for the start of the walk.

The area is well sign posted. Take the Glory Arch walk, up to the Glory Arch and South Glory Cave. The path to the Glory Cave area is well formed and makes its way along a neatly cut trail in the hillside with the limestone cliffs a feature on the other side of the gully. After visiting the South Glory Cave, retrace your steps back along the Glory Arch Walk to a break in the fence on the right and the signposted River Walk.

Descend the River Walk and make your way along the river and to the thermal pool in the Rules Creek Valley at the far end of the trail. The Thermal Pool is a great place for a swim. The Yarrangobilly River also provides a great place to explore, paddle and picnic.

The climb out of the river is the most challenging of this walk with elevation gain of 110 metres in the last kilometre.

Closest Town: Adaminaby / Tumut

Start Location: Glory Cave Carpark, Yarrangobilly Caves Road, Yarrangobilly.

Latitude and longitude: 35.725700°S, 148.489635°E

Grade: 3

Trail Quality: Easy walk along formed trails. There are pathways into the South Glory Cave. The River Walk is steep in the final ascent out of the valley to the carpark. Signposted.

Distance: 3.2 km

Time: 2 hours 30 minutes

Amenities: Yes

Park Type: Yarrangobilly area of the Kosciuszko National Park.

South Glory Cave

Yarrangobilly Visitor Centre

Glory Hole Walk

River Walk

Yarrangobilly Caves Thermal Pool

Along the Way:

The Glory Arch – a magnificent natural archway hewn from limestone layers over millions of years.

South Glory Cave – enjoy a self-guided walk through the South Glory Cave, taking in the stalagmites, stalactites.

Hidden in the Rules Creek Valley, the **thermal pool** is a spring fed pool surrounded by towering eucalypt trees. It is a great place to relax after a hike through the caves.

Merritts Traverse Track

A challenging walk touring the Crackenback Mountain Area and discovering Merritts Traverse track. Experience the snowfields during the summer months, enjoying a chairlift to the start and some good descents to the finish. The wildflowers are in bloom from late spring and once the snow clears this is a great place to view some rare and local plants including: snow daisies, yellow billy buttons, and Kosciuszko's very own Anemone Buttercup. Weather can change quickly in Alpine regions. This walk is not open in winter months and is best walked between December and April.

Description: At just 1.9 km to the top of Mt Crackenback, Merritt's is a formidable, steep and unforgiving track. This walk reverses that by enjoying one of the unique features of the Kosciuszko National Park and takes the chairlift to the top to start the walk, before walking back down to Thredbo.

After disembarking from the chairlift, it is optional to visit Eagles Nest Restaurant where there are information boards detailing the walk. Otherwise, make a sharp left and start to walk downhill on the paved trail. Follow the signs saying 'Merritts Nature Walk' onto dirt. You will find arrows along the way directing you as you pass by large granite boulders and descend stairs to an intersection. Turn left and continue along the Merritts Traverse Track. The main valley is to your right as you travel downwards before coming to a four-way junction. Turn to your right following the track down the left of Snowgums Chairlift. Veering left and departing from the chairlift, bear steeply downhill.

The Snow Gums in this area are splendid and atmospheric, it is easy to imagine them eloquently playing host to

Closest Town: Thredbo

Start Location: Start at the Kosciuszko Express Chairlift, Friday Drive, Thredbo. Chairlift tickets are available at the office at the bottom of the lift between December and April.

Latitude and longitude: 36.503291°S, 148.303471°E

Grade: 4

Trail Quality: Formed track, steep with frequent steps, clearly signed.

Distance: 5.8 km

Time: 3 hours 30 minutes

Amenities: Yes, at the start

Park Type: Kosciuszko National Park

Merritts Traverse Track

Merritts Nature Walk

Eagles Nest
Restaurant

Merritts Nature Walk

N

300 m

Kosciuszko
Express chairlift

Thredbo R

endless snowflakes during the colder months. At the next intersection, stay to the right, descending steep steps before coming to a wooden bench in a small clearing. The track from here is very clear and again tracks downhill, with more steps and another bench to rest at.

The next section of the walk includes some metal and timber boardwalk, more steep steps, some large granite boulders to pass by and a timber ramp which makes its way to the next intersection. Turn left following the 'Merritts Traverse' sign and at the next intersection, again follow the signs. Pass by

Sponars T-Bar lower station and then the bottom of Antons T-bar. Continue straight and follow the arrow posts as it makes its way steeply uphill and past the seasonal Frostbite Café. Further uphill, passing another Merritts Traverse sign and crossing over the creek you come to the top of Gunbarrel Express Chairlift. Continue along the wide track to the intersection, follow the track right, marked Merritts Traverse. From here until the bottom of The Cruiser, arrow markers and signage show the way.

After passing the bottom of The Cruiser, follow the signs downhill with the Cruiser on your right. The trail becomes switchbacks before entering a forest of snow gums. Continue along what in winter is the Sundowner Ski Run to Friday Flats. Pass the chairlift station, and continue down to Friday Drive turning sharply right and following the footpath. Cross the bridge and pass by the Thredbo Leisure Centre and ascend the stairs on the right, just prior to the Thredbo River. Follow the footpath, crossing the metal grate and up the steps as signed. Continue to the bottom of the bobsled run, past the tennis courts making your way around the buildings back to Kosciuszko Express chairlift and the finish of the walk.

Along the Way:

Eagle Nest Restaurant is the highest restaurant in Australia and is open year-round.

A well-placed seat on Merritts Traverse Track gives views north through the gully where water trickles along the creek and over the rocks.

The **Gunbarrel Express Chairlift Station** provides shelter and views, it's a good place to stop and refresh on this steep and challenging walk.

Thredbo Bobsled is open year-round and offers summer mountain descents on a 700-metre-long luge style track.

There are over 200 species of Alpine flowering plants that line the landscape of the alpine areas during late spring and early summer. The endangered Broad toothed rat and the corroboree frog are just some of the species reliant on the many plants native to the area.

Bullocks Track to Bullocks Hut

From Thredbo diggings campground, this easy walk is steeped in nature and history. From passing seemingly carefree wallabies and kangaroos to observing fish and platypus in the clear mountain waters of the Thredbo River, this walk is enchanting and relaxing. Bullocks Hut sits at the junctions of Little Thredbo River and Thredbo River and was built as a holiday cottage for Dr H Bullock to indulge his passion of fishing. There is plenty to explore around the hut grounds with the buildings being is superb condition.

Description: From Thredbo Diggings Campground, make your way onto Bullocks Track as it starts to hug the Thredbo River and make it's way downstream. The river is on your left the entire way to Bullocks Hut. The trail is formed and mostly flat with various bridges crossing small creeks and waterways as you travel along. At times, large granite boulders line the pathway, and there are clear views into the crystal waters of the Thredbo River. Intersections are signposted and grassy clearings give way to paved pathway as you pass under the bridge following the signs to Bullocks Hut.

After the bridge and past the junction where Little Thredbo River runs into Thredbo River, there are some relics in the paddocks just prior to Bullocks Hut.

Bullocks Hut is an enchanting place to look around. The hut stands proudly and is used for private functions. The stables are in good condition and there are various buildings to explore. Retrace your steps back to the Thredbo Diggings Campground to finish.

Closest Town: Thredbo

Start Location: Thredbo Diggings campground, Alpine Way, Kosiuszko National Park, 23 km west of Jindabyne and 14 km east of Thredbo.

Latitude and longitude: 36.447165°S, 148.425341°E

Grade: 3

Trail Quality: Occasional steps, formed track. Some obstacles. Clearly signposted.

Distance: 5 km

Time: 2 hours

Amenities: Yes, at the start

Park Type: Kosciuszko National Park

Along the Way:

Built in 1934, Bullocks Hut, located near Bullocks Flat and the junction of little Thredbo River and Thredbo River was

built for Dr H Bullock for the purpose of a holiday cottage. Dr Bullock was a passionate fisherman and the hut proved to be well placed for his leisurely pursuits.

The Thredbo river is teaming with fish, as you make your way downstream, the clear waters make it easy to spot fish swimming against the flow of the water. If you are keen, take your fishing rod for a spot of fishing where Dr Bullock once fished.

Wildlife in the area includes an abundance of wallabies and kangaroos and on dawn or dusk the enchanting Platypus, one of the most unusual creatures in the world can be seen working away in the ponds of the river.

N

200 m

Bullocks Hut

Thredbo River

Thredbo Diggings Campground

The Porcupine Rocks Walk

Views of Perisher Valley, Mount Duncan and the picturesque Thredbo River valley await. Journey through the snow gum forests, past intriguing granite tors and onto Porcupine Rocks. The views in all directions are stunning and the hovering haze created by snow gums line the mountainsides for miles in each direction.

Description: Leaving the carpark, make your way across Rock Creek on the metal footbridge and turn right following the 'Porcupine Track' signs. The track makes its way past the pumphouse and onwards past the reservoir. The trail from here is narrow, recessed into the earth and tracking uphill slightly at all times. Snow Poles stretch across the grasslands and the track again crosses Rock Creek before coming to an intersection. Stay left to continue along the Porcupine Track in a south-west direction up the valley. The next intersection indicates to continue straight towards the large granite pinnacle which is Porcupine Rocks. As you get closer the incline increases and the rocky outcrops appear to multiply. Continue straight until the track swings left and then it is a rock scramble to the top of Porcupine Rocks.

Closest Town: Perisher Village

Start Location: Galaxia Place, Perisher Valley. Park at the water supply carpark at the end.

Latitude and longitude: 36.410846°S, 148.410117°E

Grade: 3

Trail Quality: Some boardwalk and metal grate to walk along, obstacles underfoot at times, rock scrambles toward the pinnacle of Porcupine Rocks. Clearly signposted.

Distance: 5.7 km

Time: 2 hours

Amenities: No

Park Type: Kosciuszko National Park

Retrace your steps to return to the carpark. Do not follow the Porcupine Link Track. While it is enticingly named, it is not the correct trail.

Along the Way:

From the top of the Granite Tors and boulders which make up the Porcupine Rocks, there are views of Perisher Valley, Mount Duncan at 1478 metres elevation and along the Thredbo River Valley.

Wildflowers along the way are plentiful with yellow paper daisies and billy buttons showing out throughout early summer.

While the views are amazing, the area is exposed, and the rock faces can be slippery when wet.

Pheasants Peak Walking Track

Littered with impressive granite tors and under cover of old growth eucalypts, exertion is rewarded with spectacular views of the Monaro plains toward the Snowy Mountains. Sunset on the summit is just reward for a challenging walk. Be sure to pick a clear day as when the mists descend into the forest, while the smells and sounds may be reward enough, the views will be non-existent.

Description: An information board guides walkers from the carpark on to the start of the Pheasants Peak Walking Track. Starting along a rarely used firetrail, walkers will catch glimpses of the views in the distance as they pass through various species of eucalypt forests. White Ash and Brown Barrel are most dominant. If you find any parts of the walk tedious, your mind will be easily sustained by the impressive granite tors and further gratified by your ability to imagine how they came to be.

Closest Town: Bombala

Start Location: In the Coolangubra section of the South East Forest National Park, the Pheasants Peak track head is located on Waratah Way. There is parking at the track head.

Latitude and longitude: 37.019212°S, 149.401498°E

Grade: 4

Trail Quality: The first 2 km of the track is fire trail and easily traversed. Onwards walkers will encounter some rock scrambling, narrow trail and at times some seasonally overgrown areas.

Distance: 4 km

Time: 2 hours return

Amenities: No

Park Type: South East Forest National Park

The walk is direct and easily followed.

Along the Way: Granite tors, tall eucalypts and vast views across the Monaro plains.

South East Forest
National Park

Wog Way

Waratah Rd

N

400 m

Waterfall Walk

An enjoyable exploration in Kosciuszko National Park awaits with this walk starting at Sawpit Creek Picnic Area. Sawpit Creek, named after the milling of Alpine Ash in the area during the 1860s, flows by the picnic area and the Waterfall Walk leads to a serene and picturesque cascading waterfall on Upper Sawpit Creek. While the Falls are unnamed, they remain the highlight of the walk which includes clusters of large granite boulders, gully crossings and the clear trickling waters of Sawpit Creek.

Description: Leaving Sawpit Creek Picnic Area, make your way along the paved path through the road underpass. Emerging from the tunnel, make your way across the clearing to the National Parks direction marker at the intersection and continue straight, tracking into the bushland. The next landmark is a metal crossing over a small gully followed by a metal pathway. The track then leads up the hillside and along the valley through tall eucalypt forest, ascending several sets of steps before coming to the Waterfall Lookout.

To get closer to the falls, descend the metal steps and down to the creek crossing below the waterfall. The walk continues in a circuit from here back

Closest Town: Jindabyne

Start Location: Sawpit Creek Picnic Area, 1400 Kosciuszko Road, Jindabyne.

Latitude and longitude: 36.350274°S, 148.564005°E

Grade: 3

Trail Quality: Single track, steep in places, obstacles under foot, some steps and metal grates to walk on. Signposted.

Distance: 5.8 km

Time: 2 hours 30 minutes

Amenities: Yes, at the start

Park Type: Kosciuszko National Park

to Sawpit Creek. Follow the track to the right along the metal pathway as it leaves the valley. The track becomes dirt and leads away from the valley and through eucalypt forest, crossing Sawpit Creek and making its way through several gully crossings and to a large granite outcrop. Continue through the granite boulders and pass several more clusters of granite boulders before tracking downhill, to where the track turns right. Pass between the split granite boulder and continue through the forest and eventually up some stone steps and across Sawpit Creek at the bridge. Now situated next to Kosciuszko Road, make your way across the clearing and through the underpass and back to Sawpit Creek picnic area to finish.

Along the Way:

Sawpit Creek Picnic Area is a quiet picnic area equipped with wood barbeques, amenities and open spaces. The peaceful Sawpit Creek flows by and there are information signs detailing the historical significance of the area.

The unnamed waterfall is around 4 metres high and includes some cascades which add a little more height. The lookout gives a great view of the falls however the special part of the walk is getting down up close to the falls on the metal walkway.

Granite outcrops always seem to intrigue. The shapes and size, dotted across the landscape definitely add some beauty to the area and in the very least provoke the imagination. Passing through the split boulder along the walk is a treat especially for younger walkers.

Yerong Walking Track

Standing in stark contrast to the flat farmlands on the Riverina plains, a rugged rock outcrop that can be seen from the passing highway, The Rock is an intriguing part of the landscape. The Rock which stands 364 metres above the plains and once served as a ceremonial site for the Wiradjuri people, it was a Dreaming place and lookout and known as Kengal meaning 'Sloping Hill'. The walk to the summit is challenging and steep in places but the trail is well defined.

Description: From the start, the Yerong Walking track is signposted and easy to follow. Walking first through a relatively flat section and through cypress pine forest, the trail leads south, following the summit ridgeline. The flat trail doesn't last long and soon the Yerong Track zigzags up the hill steeply until you reach the base of cliffs below the summit. Continue along the track again trending south. The track corners back and continues to climb on the south western side and along large rock shelves. The views of the Riverina plains and the connecting ridgeline become more visible from this point onwards and it is worth resting just to take in the varying vistas.

Closest Town: The Rock

Start Location: Kengal (The Rock) Picnic Area, The Rock Access Road off The Rock-Lockhart Road, The Rock. The walk starts near the information shelter.

Latitude and longitude: 35.261101°S, 147.075768°E

Grade: 3

Trail Quality: Formed track, some obstacles, short steep hills, steps. Clearly signposted.

Distance: 6 km

Time: 3 hours 30 minutes

Amenities: Yes, at the start

Park Type: The Rock Nature Reserve – Kengal Aboriginal Place

The track doubles back and up another rock ledge to the summit. Retrace your steps to return to the finish at (Kengal) The Rock Picnic Area.

Along the Way:

Along the way you will find information signs detailing the history of the Wiradjuri people and the European settlers who later made their lives in the area.

Prior to the summit you pass a stand of Wooly Ragwort plants. These are a threatened species which are native to the area, and the largest stand of these plants in the world. In spring they bloom with yellow flowers.

The Rock has had several names over time. Traditionally the Wiradjuri people called The Rock *Kengal*, meaning sloping hill. European settlers to the area christened it 'The Hanging Rock' due to the pronounced overhang on its eastern side. It was renamed 'The Rock' after the overhang collapsed in 1874.

From 1891, the lower slopes of The Rock were quarried to provide ballast material for the Sydney to Melbourne rail line.

The Rock, which sits at the northern end of a small range, is the result of a pressure uplift of sedimentary materials. The Rock Nature Reserve – Kengal Aboriginal Place, sits on the border of the Riverina Plains and Western Slopes. The diversity of landscape is reflected back in the flora and fauna that inhabit the area.

On a clear day, Mount Kosciuszko is visible as is the mountains of the Victorian alps.

Yindyamarra Sculpture Walk

Yindyamarra is an aboriginal word derived from the Wiradjuri language, it means respect, be gentle, be polite and do slowly. The Yindyamarra Sculpture Walk is a 5 kilometre figure eight loop featuring 15 sculptures and 10 painted panels. The sculptures, each tell a story or represent an important part of culture and experience and were crafted at times in collaboration and at times solo by local aboriginal artists.

Description: Starting on the Murray River, this walk heads west to the first sculpture, titled *Teaming Life of Milawa Billa*, onto *Reconciliation Shield* and then *Creature Seats*, from which you turn left and take the path that continues to hug the Murray River. Along this stretch of the walk *Googar* and *Wiradjuri Women* feature, and the pathway walk is peaceful as it makes its way against the flow of the Murray.

The next part of the walk links to the second loop and features *Vertical Message Sticks* and at *Bogong Moth Migration* the pathway splits, take the left option. The next sculptures are close together and you pass the *Maya Fish Trap*, *Goanna*, *Leaving our Mark* and *Celebrate Together*. At the site of *Celebrate Together* the trail forks. To the left is a short walk to the installation *The Bigger Picture*. After viewing *The Bigger Picture*, return to *Celebrate Together* and turn left and continue around Horseshoe Lagoon to *Family Gathering*. The pathway continues to *Bogong Moth Migration* and after passing *Vertical Message Sticks* take the left at the fork and make your way toward *Guguburra*. *Guguburra* is the last of the sculptures and you then pass previously viewed sculptures before returning to Kremur Street Boat Ramp and picnic area.

Closest Town: Albury

Start Location: Kremur Street Boat Ramp, end of Kremur Street, West Albury.

Latitude and longitude: 36.087193°S, 146.889497°E

Grade: 2

Trail Quality: 2-metre-wide sealed pathway. Clearly signposted.

Distance: 5 km

Time: 3 hours

Amenities: Yes, at the start

Park Type: Urban

Along the Way:

The sculptures each feature an information plaque with details of the inspiration and artists behind the creative piece. While some are inspired by land and culture, some are inspired by personal journey and experience. Each piece is unique.

There are opportunities to extend your walk in both directions. Continuing west along the pathway from *The Bigger Picture* leads to the Wonga Wetlands which contains excellent bird watching opportunities and 3 pathways of varying lengths to explore. Continuing east along the pathway from Kremur Street boat ramp along the Murray River leads to the beautiful Noreuil Park in Albury with excellent family facilities to enjoy.

North East

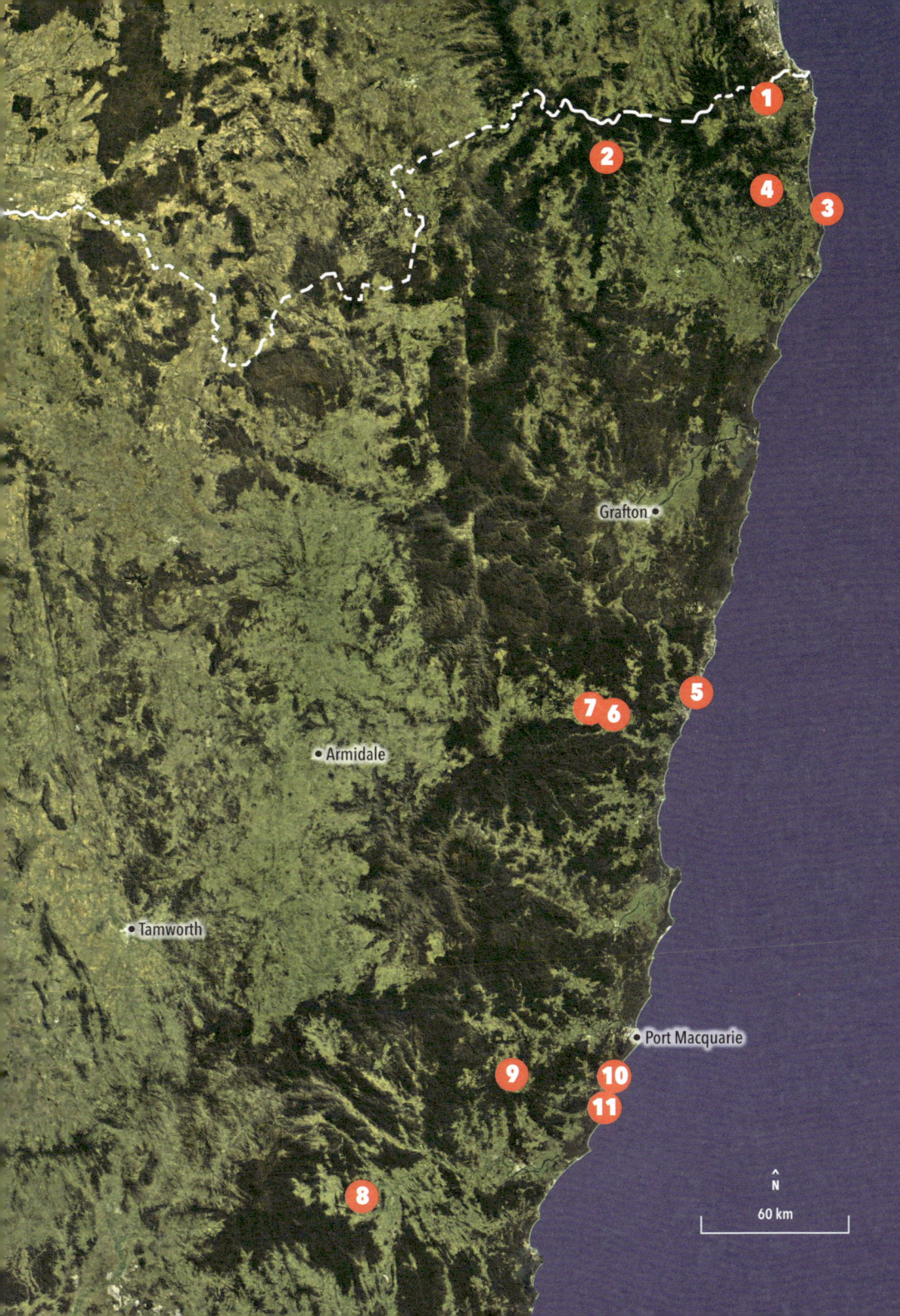

Grafton

Armidale

Tamworth

Port Macquarie

1

2

4

3

5

7 6

9

10

11

8

N

60 km

Bar Mountain Circuit and Beech Glade

Sporting views of Mount Barney and Mount Lindesay, you could be forgiven for thinking the dramatic views of these mountains are the gem in the crown of this walk. However, the contrasting cool temperate and warm temperate rainforests provide ample intrigue as you traverse from one to another and on to the high point of the lookout. Covered in moss, the Antarctic Beech trees of the Beech Glade Walk are breath-taking. Combined with other cool temperate rainforest flora including the stunning *Falcorostrum* Orchids which sit high up on Antarctic Beech branches, this short walk engages the senses with temperature changes, sights and smells.

Description: Starting at Bar Mountain Picnic Area, the Bar Mountain Circuit Walk begins by heading west.

Descending into the ancient cool temperate rainforest, listen for Lyrebirds in this area as they busily scratch among the leaf litter on the rainforest floor. While Lyrebirds can often be heard, it may take some quiet patience to spot one of these shy birds. As you descend further, the cool temperate rainforest gives way to the warm temperate rainforest and the foliage changes to more slender trees such as coachwood and tree ferns. Leaving the warm temperate rainforest, make your way through the eucalypt forest, most notable for its Blackbutt trees and on to the Bar Mountain lookout which is at the most western point of the track.

Closest Town: Kyogle

Start Location: Bar Mountain Picnic Area, Bar Mountain Road, Upper Horseshoe Creek. 200m west of the intersection of Bar Mountain Road and Tweed Range Scenic Drive. The picnic area is 41 km from Kyogle.

Latitude and longitude: 28.459058°S, 153.132285°E

Grade: 3

Trail Quality: Formed track, some obstacles underfoot, steps and some short steep sections. The track is clearly marked and easily followed.

Distance: 5 km

Time: 3 hours

Amenities: Yes – at the start

At the lookout, Mt Barney, Mt Lindesay and the Border Ranges, which were all once part of the ancient Tweed Volcano can be seen in the distance.

Leave the lookout and continue along the route back to the carpark where the Beech Glade walk starts.

While just a short walk, the Beech Glade walk offers a look at some of the large, majestic and ancient Antarctic Beech trees, some of which are thought to be over 2000 years old. The branches of the Antarctic Beech give habitat to the magnificent *Falcorostrum* Orchid. The area is teaming with fern life including birds nest ferns and staghorn. The walk is signposted and returns to the carpark. It is a worthwhile addition to the Bar Mountain Circuit as the ancient Gondwana Rainforest is on display throughout the walk.

Along the Way:

Through the Beech Glade walk, the *Falcorostrum* Orchid can be found on random branches of the Antarctic Beech Tree.

The rainforests throughout the area have been deemed World Heritage areas and are part of Australia's magnificent surviving Gondwana Rainforest.

Bar Mountain Lookout

Border Ranges National Park

N

200 m

Bar Mountain Picnic Area

Beech Glade

Murray Scrub Walking Track

An assault on the senses, the Murray Scrub Walking Track boasts sights sounds and smells that will leave you feeling alive and engaged. Everything in the park feels enormous, from the magnificent stand of old growth cedar trees to the towering bungalow palms and the tremendous strangler figs. The rainforest is rich and diverse with foliage of palms, strangler figs and ferns just some of what awaits on this walk. With such diverse and rich vegetation, the wildlife, lizards and birds easily find habitat and food and sightings are common.

Description: The Murray Scrub Trackhead is signposted from the Murray Scrub carpark. Initially the track is challenging with tree roots making formidable obstacles especially if it has been raining as they are quite slippery. After approximately 1.5 km, take the option to the right at the track junction. This next section of the walk is a loop and is approximately 1.9 km. Once in the loop, enjoy the stand of old growth cedar trees in the northern part of the loop which are a highlight of the walk. Continue around the loop, through the thick rainforest with the lagoon on the left. In dry times the lagoon resembles a grassy field. As you reach the next junction, veer to the right and continue straight along the trail to the Murray Scrub Carpark and the finish.

Along the Way:

Murray Scrub Lookout is just a short drive along Toonumbar Forest Drive. The views over the rainforest are spectacular with views out to Glassy Mountain (920m) and Dome Mountain (915m). Information boards at the lookout detail the areas history as the Focal Peak shield volcano.

Closest Town:
Toonumbar

Start Location: Murray Scrub walking track carpark, Murray Scrub Road, Toonumbar. 37 km north west of Kyogle.

Latitude and longitude:
28.51793358°S,
152.7706661°E

Grade: 3

Trail Quality: Short steep hills, many obstacles under foot, many steps. Clearly signposted.

Distance: 5.5 km

Time: 2 hours 30 minutes

Amenities: None nearby

Park Type: Toonumbar National Park

The Toonumbar National Park is part of the Githabul Nation native claim which was first lodged in 1995. In 2007 a consent determination was made in the Federal Court of Australia recognising the Githabul peoples native title rights in nine national parks and 13 state forests in the northern New South Wales area. The consent determination recognises native title rights and also protects the rights of other parties.

Rare bird species including the White-Eared Monarchs and the Wompoo Fruit Dove can be found in the park. Sooty Owls also make their home in the area.

Cape Byron Walking Track

A walk along one of the most pristine stretches of populated coastline on the eastern seaboard of Australia. Half a day spent in this area confirms that the Byron Bay area is truly special and justifiably a mecca for the rich and famous. Views from different vantage points along the walk allow you to gaze into the mesmerising waters and spot all manner of sea life from frolicking dolphins to graceful stingrays and the ancient wise sea turtles. The views, the landscape and the marine life make this an interesting and intriguing walk.

Description: Starting at the picnic area facing Clarkes Beach, follow the Cape Byron Walking Track as it makes its way north east along boardwalk. At the end of the boardwalk , veer left and follow the track through bushland to the outdoor seating at **The Pass Café**. Veer left again, and from the cafe take the stairs to the left and down past the picnic tables to the entry to the sand at The Pass. Walking down onto the sand, make your way to the right and across the sand to the island-like headland. Steps climb the small island to the viewing platform of Fisherman's Lookout with clear views out to Julian Rocks.

Closest Town: Byron Bay

Start Location: Captain Cook Lookout and picnic area, opposite 130 Lighthouse Road, Byron Bay.

Latitude and longitude: 28.642086°S, 153.625920°E

Grade: 3

Trail Quality: Boardwalk, paved pathway and some unsealed trail to the summit. Some sand walking. Many steps. Some obstacles underfoot on the return trip. Signposted.

Distance: 4.2 km

Time: 2 hours 30 minutes

Amenities: Yes, at the start

Park Type: Cape Byron State Conservation Area

Retrace your steps off the sand and stay left as you walk up the boat launch area. The pathway is to your left and unsealed for a short distance, before passing a large information board on the left and becoming paved. Shortly after the track splits. Take the paved option to the left, along Cape Byron Walking Track, staying close to the ocean. The track hugs the coastline, with Marine Parade on your right. Pass the foreshore of Wategoes Beach and at the end of the beach stay left as the pathway diverges from Marine

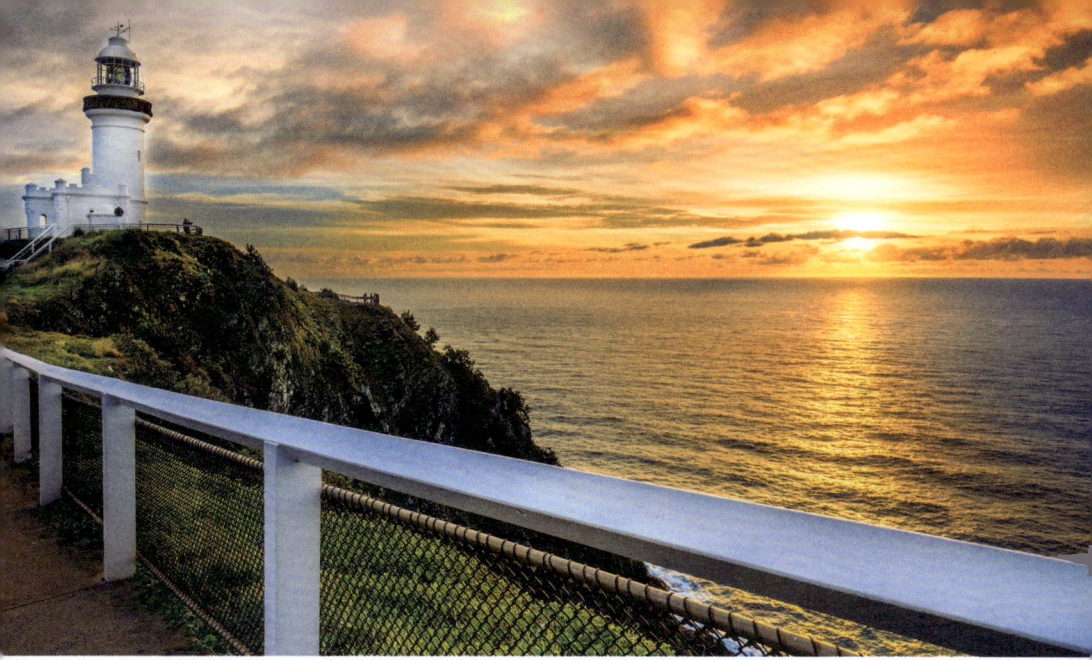

Parade and makes its way into the bush and around the headland. Parts of the track are boardwalk and parts are paved as the path reaches a track to the left marked with directional signage to Little Wategoes Beach. There is a side trip out to Cape Byron. Turn left here, taking the steps down toward Little Wategoes Beach and on to Cape Byron viewing platform. Retrace your steps back to the main trail and turn left, now trending south along Cape Byron Walking Track.

Continue to the viewing platform and then along the paved track as the lighthouse comes into sight. Climbing the last steps to the lighthouse, this is a great place for a break and to take in the ambience of the location, the blue waters and the strong scent of the ocean. In colder months whales can be seen migrating north and dolphin pods commonly play off the cape. On clear days, stingrays and sea turtles can also be seen.

Pass by the lighthouse staying left as you descend past the lighthouse keepers cottage and out of the lighthouse precinct. The pathway hugs the road for 300 metres, then diverges from the road and into the bushland where it becomes the unsealed Tallows Ridge Track. Continue down Tallow Ridge Track, in and out of the tree canopy. Depending on the tree cover, there are commanding views to the beaches south of Byron Bay. There are lots of steps in this part of the track as it descends off the headland. As you leave the tree cover and exit the trail, turn left and walk to the junction of Lighthouse Road. Cross Lighthouse Road, finding yourself back at Captain Cook parking area and the finish.

Along the Way:

Fisherman's Lookout – located on the rocky outcrop at The Pass. The Pass is a beach north of Clarkes Beach and famous with surfers worldwide. The viewing platform at Fishermans Lookout is a great place to look through the clear ocean waters and spot dolphins, sea turtles and stingrays.

Cape Byron Lighthouse – built in 1901, the 22 metre high lighthouse tower loyally stands guard over Cape Byron and the most easterly point of Australia. The lighthouse precinct also hosts a number of cottages for holiday letting and a maritime museum detailing the history and significance of the area.

Whales, Whales, Whales! From various viewing platforms along Cape Byron Walking Track, and during the colder months of June and July Humpback and Southern Right Whales head north to the warmer waters to calve. In September and November they make their way south again, with their young in tow to feed in the southern oceans. It is a truly exhilarating experience to spot some migrating whales and they are at times prone to some theatrics!

Rummery Park to Minyon Falls Lookout

From the picturesque grounds of Rummery Park campground, this walk meanders through sub-tropical rainforest and alongside Repentance Creek. Pass by the Repentance Creek Cascades and onward to the viewing deck at the top of Minyon Falls. Views into the gorge below and at the falling waters of Minyon Falls as they make their way 100 metres over rhyolite cliffs are spectacular.

Description: From Rummery Park, the entrance to Boggy Creek Track is signposted.

The Boggy Creek Trail winds through sub-tropical rainforest, making its way along the banks of Boggy Creek. There are information signs along the way detailing the vegetation in the area. Keeping the creek on your right, continue on past the Boggy Creek cascades to where the trail meets the boardwalk. Track right at the next junction and continue along the

Closest Town: Dunoon

Start Location: Rummery Park campground, Peates Mountain Road, Whian Whian.

Latitude and longitude: 28.598937°S, 153.378218°E.

16 km north of Dunoon.

Grade: 3

Trail Quality: Narrow bush trail, some obstacles under foot, very boggy in places. Rocks can be extremely slippery. Boardwalk in places. Clearly signposted.

Distance: 4 km

Time: 1 hour 30 minutes

Amenities: Yes

Park Type: Whian Whian State Conservation Area

boardwalk. At the next intersection, again track right to the Minyon Falls viewing platform.

Retrace your steps to return to Rummery Park.

Along the Way:

Minyon Falls, on Repentance Creek is a plunge waterfall, with waters dropping over rhyolite cliffs, more than 100 metres to the rocks below.

Whian Whian State Conservation Area is a haven for a diverse population of wildlife including lace monitors, peregrine falcons, red-eyed green tree frogs, carpet pythons and green tree snakes. Koalas, pademelons and long-nosed bandicoots have also been sighted.

Flora in the area includes an array of ferns and vegetation consistent with sub-tropical rainforest. In addition, wet sclerophyll forest forms the forest canopy providing a diverse habitat as evidenced by the diverse wildlife that populate the area.

Rummery Park campground was originally a camp for forestry workers who were logging highly sought-after Red Cedar Trees in the Whian Whian area. While Cedar was stripped from the forests as early as the 1830s, Rummery Park was utilised from the 1930s onwards when the road network was more conducive to extracting the logs.

Muttonbird Island Nature Reserve Walk

The walk up and over Muttonbird Island offers a unique perspective of the Coffs Harbour area. From the Eastern Side Lookout, the views are ocean vistas over Solitary Islands Marine Park. At the peak of Muttonbird Island you can look back across the city of Coffs Harbour, the marina and beaches. In the distance you get coastal views as far as South West Rocks and Woolgoolga and inland to the impressive mountainous ranges. The award winning Muttonbird Island outdoor learning space provides detail about the significance of the island to both the Gumbaynggirr Aboriginal people and local conservation.

Description: This walk starts at the Jetty park carpark. Walking along the breakwater toward the marina, the path is all sealed and clear to follow. Make your way past the marina on your right keeping the ocean on your left.

Pass by the mesmerising cove at the foot of Muttonbird Island with its eddies and swirling waters crashing against the rocks. Continue onto the island and to the Muttonbird Island outdoor learning space. This space details indigenous history, dreamtime stories and conservation efforts. From the education centre the pathway across the island is paved and steep. Part way up the climb there is a resting place, after a quick stop continue on to the first viewing platform.

Leaving the viewing platform, continue along the paved track to the Eastern Side lookout and the halfway point of the walk.

Retrace your steps to return to the finish.

Closest Town: Coffs Harbour

Start Location: Coffs Harbour Jetty Park, Marina Drive near the corner of Jordan Esplanade, Coffs Harbour.

Latitude and longitude: 30.302253°S, 153.141318°E

Grade: 3

Trail Quality: Sealed pathway with some steep sections and a few steps on Muttonbird Island. Clearly signposted.

Distance: 3 km

Time: 1 hour 30 minutes

Amenities: Yes, located in the Jetty Park.

Park Type: Muttonbird Island Nature Reserve

Along the Way:

Muttonbird Island outdoor learning space is based at the foot of Muttonbird Island Nature Reserve and details the Gumbaynggirr Aboriginal people and their history with the island. Further information is detailed about the conservation efforts as you make your way across the island.

Muttonbird Island Nature Reserve is an important breeding ground for the Wedge-Tailed Shearwater (Muttonbirds). These migratory birds make their way from Asia every august to nest and breed on Muttonbird Island. There are information boards along the walk that detail the lifecycle of the muttonbirds.

Humpback Whales can be seen between May and November annually as they make their annual migration north to mate and calve.

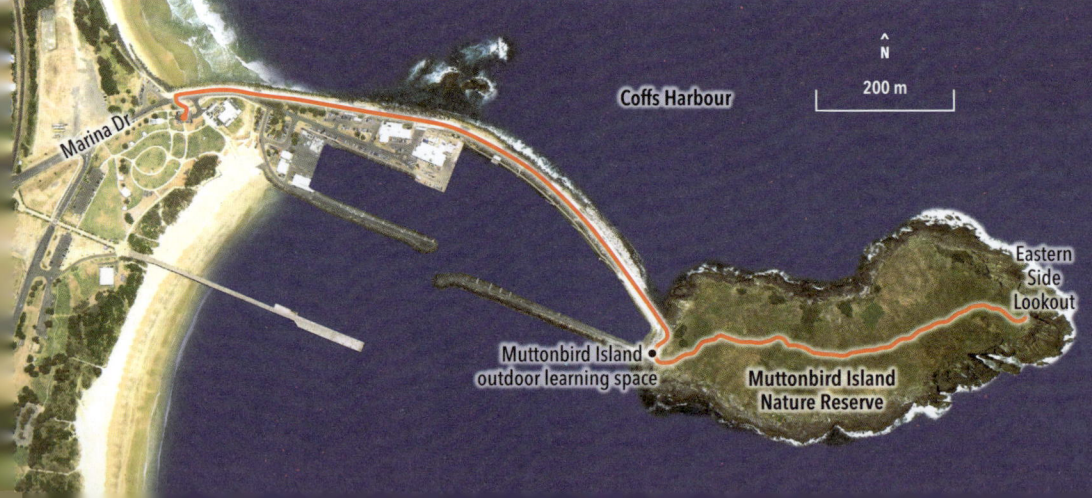

Wonga Walk

One of the most popular walks on earth, The Wonga Walk loops through the tall, lush, subtropical and World-Heritage-listed rainforest. This walk contrasts the liveliness of an ancient rainforest with the calm relaxation of its sights and sounds. The rainforest is brimming with activity, from the waterways to the lush undergrowth, coloured fungi and the canopy above, there are layers to take in and much to cast an intrigued eye over. The sounds are that of a complex and talented orchestra, shrill birds, waterfalls, trickling streams, excited chatter from fellow walkers and the rustling of a lyrebird's important work being conducted, again layers to take in.

To take the Wonga Walk is to stroll among 600-year-old trees, to follow the sounds of the waterways and to take in as much serenity as is possible in a day.

Description: Maps are available from the Dorrigo Rainforest Centre.

Starting at the Dorrigo Rainforest Centre, make your way 400 metres

Park Type: Dorrigo National Park

Closest Town: Dorrigo

Start Location: Dorrigo Rainforest Centre, 142 Dome Road, Dorrigo Mountain. 3.5 km south of the town of Dorrigo.

Latitude and longitude: 30.363561°S, 152.728468°E

Grade: 2

Trail Quality: Formed track, some elevated boardwalk, some steps, steep inclines and boulder crossings. Clearly signposted.

Distance: 6.6 km

Time: 2 hours 30 minutes

Amenities: Yes, at the Centre

along the Lyrebird Link Track to join the Wonga Walk. From here the walk does a loop of 5.8 km, taking in various waterfalls and notable landmarks before returning to where you left the Lyrebird Link Track, and then back to the Dorrigo Rainforest Centre. The Wonga Walk is clearly signposted at junctions and easy to follow. The map from the Dorrigo Rainforest Centre is informative and well worth picking up before you walk.

The Dorrigo Rainforest Centre is open 7 days from 9am until 4:30pm daily.

Along the Way:

There are several waterfalls along the Wonga Walk including, most notably, Crystal Shower Falls. A suspension bridge leads to the Falls where you can

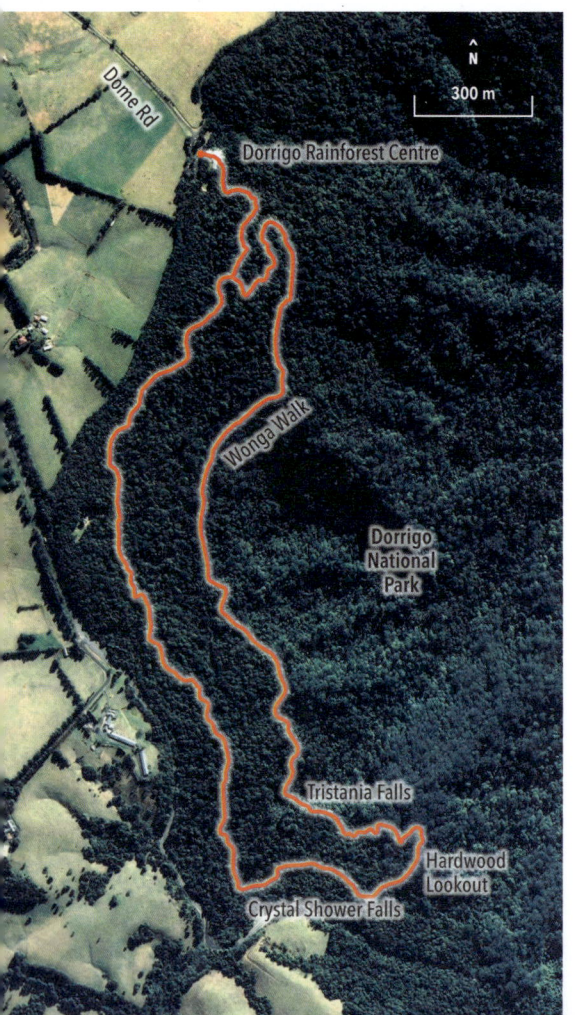

enter the cavern behind and look out through the tumbling waters. If entered at night, the cavern is known to light up with glow worms.

The elevated boardwalk gives a bird's eye view of the rainforest and its ancient trees. Look for the southern angle-headed dragon on some of the ancient tree trunks as you pass by.

Hardwood Lookout casts south with views across the Dorrigo National Park. There is a restful bench to sit and contemplate on.

Tristania Falls flows year-round and is another 30-minute walk on from Crystal Shower Falls. A footbridge takes you across the front of Tristania Falls which cascades out of the hillside.

Red Cedar Falls Walking Track

A challenging Grade 5 walk, this walk makes its way through the World Heritage Listed rainforest of the Dorrigo National Park to Red Cedar Falls. Red Cedar Falls is the largest waterfall in the area. The walk is challenging and rewarded with dramatic views of the famed Red Cedar Falls.

Description: From the Never Never Picnic Area, follow the signs for the Rosewood Creek Walking Track. After 2 km, turn left onto the Red Cedar Falls Walking Track and make your way another 1.2 km into the valley. This

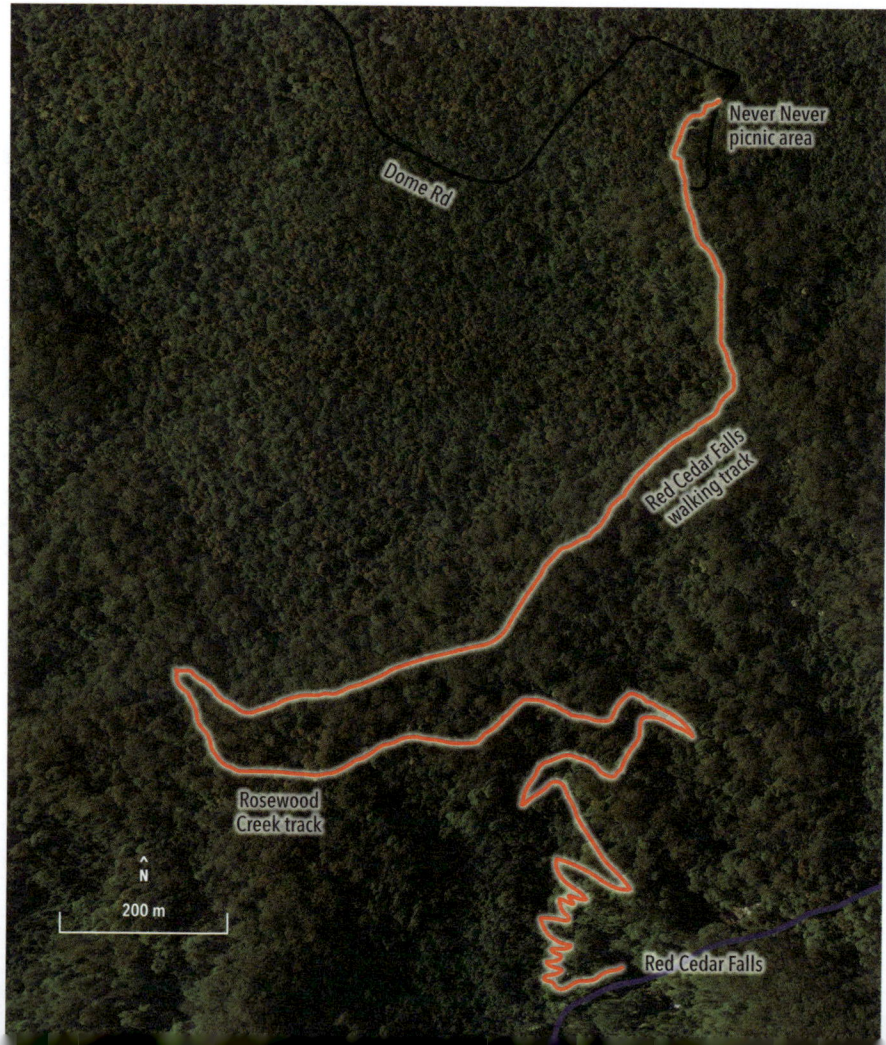

Closest Town: Dorrigo

Start Location: Never Never Picnic Area. From the Waterfall Way, enter Dome Road and continue past the Dorrigo Rainforest Centre for approximately 10 km to the end of Dome Road. Parking is at the Never Never Picnic ground.

Latitude and longitude: 30.3614953°S, 152.7985841°E

Grade: 5

Trail Quality: Formed track, some obstacles, very steep and often difficult ascent/descent. Clearly signposted.

Distance: 8 km

Time: 3 hours 30 minutes

Amenities: Yes, at Never Never Picnic Ground

Park Type: Dorrigo National Park

part of the trail descends steeply. Allow the thunderous sounds of the waterfalls to guide you as you come into sight of the largest waterfall in the Dorrigo National Park. The sight of the Red Cedar Waterfall is truly magnificent, and the roar of the waters as they tumble into the valley below is imposing.

Retrace your steps ascending the Red Cedar Walking Track and turning right onto Rosewood Creek Walking track. Make your way back to the Never Never Picnic Area.

Along the Way:

Red Cedar Falls – the largest waterfall in the Dorrigo National Park.

Hidden Treasure Track

Take a walk-through gold mining history along the Hidden Treasure Track. Remnants of mining machinery, abandoned as the gold deposits disappeared remain in the bushland, marking a prosperous time in history. In addition, the flora and fauna of the area is spectacular with strangler figs, dry rainforest and eucalypts all providing habitat for a myriad of mammals and birdlife. Koalas can be spotted in the tall eucalypts, peacefully grazing or sleeping.

Description: From Copeland Tops Picnic Area, the walk heads west and uphill along the unsealed Old Copeland Road, then heads quickly into the bush. The trail is well signposted and easily followed. At the first fork, veer left and continue. Crossing over Copeland Creek several times and eventually coming to another fork in the trail, again veer left. From here, the trail is a loop and continues around until it re-joins the trail back to the picnic area. The trail passing mining relics, an old boiler and adits (tunnelled entrances to underground mines) all a reminder of the history of mining in the area. The Basin Walk comes in from the left part way around the loop. At this point continue to the right, making your way back to the intersection where you veer left and retrace your steps to the picnic area.

Closest Town: Copeland

Start Location: Hidden Treasure Picnic Area, Copeland Road, Copeland. 1.4 km south east of the intersection of Scone Road and Copeland Road.

Latitude and longitude: 32.001941°S, 151.833732°E

Grade: 3

Trail Quality: Flat, formed track, some steps, clearly signposted.

Distance: 4.5 km

Time: 2 hours

Amenities: Yes, at the start

Park Type: Copeland Tops State Conservation Area

Along the Way:

Adits – can be spotted throughout the forest. Far from their intended use, adits now provide passage for populations of microbats as they make their way into and out of the caves.

Gold was discovered in the Hidden Treasure area in 1876. Once word spread of the discovery, over 800 miners descended on the area and a township of 1100

people formed. Three pubs and four stores were built and catered for the needs of the population. After construction of the mines, 269 kilograms of gold was mined making it one of the most productive mines in the area.

Hidden Treasure Picnic Area is the meeting point for Mountain Maid Gold Mine Guided Tours. Booking are essential: 1300 072 757 (https:// www.nationalparks.nsw.gov.au/things-to-do/guided-tours/mountain-maid-gold-mine-tour).

Koalas are among the wildlife that frequent the Copeland Tops State Conservation Area and can be spotted in the Eucalypt Forests. Birdlife such as the Wompoo Fruit-Doves, Australia's largest dove and the Glossy Glack Cockatoo also make their home in the area.

Hidden Treasure track makes its way through dry rainforest landscape. Grey Myrtle, Shatterwood and yellow tulip all feature in this area.

Rawson Falls Walk

Protecting a significant remnant of six types of rainforest that once covered the Comboyne Plateau, the Boorganna Nature Reserve is the second oldest of such reserves in New South Wales. Rawson's Falls Walk offers an up-close experience of the spectacular Rawson Falls, a waterfall with a dramatic 40-metre drop, a picturesque lookout across the reserve and a tranquil plunge pool at the bottom.

Flora and Fauna in the park are plentiful and the smells of the rainforest ensure you are aware of your location.

Description: While most waterfalls are at their best after rain, the walk to Rawson's Falls is best done after rain but not heavy rain. If you intend to swim, the pool at the bottom tends to disappear under the falling waters if the rain has been heavy.

Leaving the Boorganna picnic area, follow the signs to the track head and begin your descent along the forested track. There are signs along the way to explain the rainforest you are walking through and its significance. After just 10 minutes on the trail, it feels like you are in a Jumanji movie. The vines drape low, and the trees and fallen logs play host to an amazing array of fungi. With such a rich and bountiful playground, birds can be heard throughout the walk, unperturbed by human presence.

As you come to a flatter section of the walk, the trail narrows and then starts to descend via switchbacks, keeping the gradient gentle. You cross over the creek and continue to descend to a junction which is signposted. The lookout option takes you on a 40-metre detour where you can stand on the boardwalk and look out over the forest, the falls can barely be seen

Closest Town: Comboyne, 2429

Start Location: Boorganna Picnic Area, Innes View Road, Comboyne. The turnoff is 6.5 km from the town of Comboyne.

Latitude and longitude: 31.610722°S, 152.414287°E

Grade: 4

Trail Quality: Rough Track, many obstacles under foot, many steps. Signposted.

Distance: 5 km

Time: 2 hours 30 minutes

Amenities: None at the start

Park Type: Boorganna Nature Reserve

from here but the lookout is worthwhile as it gives a great vantage point for spotting some of the many birdlife in the reserve.

Retrace your steps and take the trail to the base of the falls as signposted. It is another kilometre to the base of the falls. Descending, the roar of the water soon becomes apparent and while there are a few slippery spots on the track, it is clear to follow with good foot pads to land on. Reaching the bottom of the track, the waterfall and pool below is surrounded by large boulders, which you can easily pick you way across.

Return the way you came, ascending the trail back to the picnic area.

Along the Way:

There are information boards detailing the history of the area and points of interest about the different types of rainforest you walk through. Boorganna is one of the most diverse botanical environments in New South Wales.

Rainforests in the area include: warm temperate, subtropical, gully rainforest and wet and dry sclerophyll forest.

With over 80 species of birds, and some great vantage points to observe them from, visiting the reserve could easily become a full day out. Threatened species in the reserve include the yellow throated scrub wren, crimson rosellas, scarlet honeyeaters and rose robins.

The reserve contributes to the Tapin Tops / Killabakh wildlife corridor and with such a bounty of foliage, wildlife is content to inhabit the reserve including some vulnerable species. Yellow-Bellied Gliders, Long-Nosed Potoroos and Parma Wallabies are among the vulnerable. The Long-Nosed Bandicoot, Red-Necked Pademelon and Spotted-Tailed Quoll also inhabit the area.

Wildflowers in Spring include the spotted cinnamon orchids, and the fungi, in an array of colours, make their presence known during autumn.

Perpendicular Point and the Flower Bowl

A walk to along the exposed headland of Perpendicular Point to the most easterly point of the outcrop where whale sightings are common during migration season. Enjoy the wildflowers of the Flower Bowl Circuit, the stunning Charles Hamey and Logan lookouts and the wild and exposed Perpendicular Point viewing area. Dolphin sightings are common off this section of coastline.

Description: Starting on the Perpendicular Point Walking track, quickly turn right onto Flower Bowl Circuit and continue 1.2 km toward Charles Hamey Lookout. *Ignore the track on the right from Dunbogan Lookout and bear left.* At the next intersection, turn right and take the trail to Charles Hamey Lookout. Retrace your steps to that intersection and turn onto the Flower Bowl Circuit again, continuing along until you reach the Perpendicular Point Walk. Turn right. Another intersection shortly after directs you to continue left toward Logans Lookout and Perpendicular Point Walk.

Continue along Perpendicular Point Walk making your way along the headland to Perpendicular Point. To return, follow Perpendicular Point Walking Track all the way back to the carpark and finish, staying to the right at each intersection.

Closest Town: Camden Head

Start Location: Carpark next to 192 Camden Head Road, Camden Head, on the corner of Bergalia Crescent.

Latitude and longitude: 31.64084698°S, 152.8356952°E

Grade: 3

Trail Quality: Formed Track, some obstacles, occasional steps. Clearly signposted.

Distance: 5.1 km

Time: 2 hours 30 minutes

Amenities: None at the start. Closest is at Pilot Beach, Pilot Beach Road.

Park Type: Kattang National Park

Along the Way:

With over 123 species of birds found in the reserve, The Flower Bowl Circuit, with its spectacular wildflower display of orchids, dillwynia and boronias attract flocks of various honeyeaters. Overhead sea birds such as the Osprey and Brahminy Kites enjoy the thermals, and migratory birds are plentiful in spring and summer.

Charles Hamey lookout has a southerly aspect, looking over Gogleys Lagoon and the serene sands of Dunbogan Beach. North Brother Mountain can be clearly seen in the distance.

Perpendicular Point looks out across the crystal blue ocean and is a popular place to view whales during migration in June/July and October/November. Views extend to Port Macquarie and across Dooragan National Park to North Brother Mountain.

Perpendicular Point

Perpendicular Point walking track

Flower Bowl Circuit

Camden Head Rd

Charles Hamey Lookout

N

200 m

Diamond Head Loop Walk

Scenic coastal views, and the ever-present possibility of spotting dolphins, the Diamond Head Loop links the Headland Walking Track with the Forest Walking track taking in vast ocean vistas, heathland, forests and dry rainforest areas. The birdlife is intriguing; however, the star of this walk is the coastline, which is nothing short of spectacular. There are various places to look down from the cliffs to the rocks and waves below and view extend north and south and to the hinterland and the Three Brothers Mountains.

Description: From the campground, follow the Diamond Head Access Road leaving the campground are. Turn left at the signposted Diamond Head Loop Track. This section of the walk is formed gravel pathway and travels through open heathland with the ocean on the left. The views over the beach below are spectacular and as you gain elevation you can see down to the waves crashing on the rocks below. At the fork in the track continue along the left option, straight ahead. From here, the walk is a loop which will come out of the bush back to this spot via the track to your right.

Closest Town: Laurieton

Start Location: Diamond Head Campground, Diamond Head Road, Diamond Head. 9.5 km south of Laurieton.

Latitude and longitude: 31.718403°S, 152.794037°E

Grade: 3

Trail Quality: Short steep hills, some steps, formed trail, clearly signposted.

Distance: 4.3 km

Time: 2 hours

Amenities: Yes

Park Type: Crowdy Bay National Park

Continue the gentle climb along the headland through some taller stands of heath and to the old trig marker where you turn right and continue along the Headland walk. The track narrows for some time and continues over the headland and downhill. Part way up the following rise there is a small diversion to the left which looks out across the ocean and headlands and a view below to the aptly named Diamond Head. There are several more unofficial lookouts to explore as you continue along the track, however all are unfenced.

Pit Trail

Diamond Head Rd

Diamond Head campground

Diamond Head

Indian Head campground

N

200 m

Passing the resting bench, there is a fork in the track. The left option leads down the Arch Track to a view of the Natural Arch rock formation. Continue to your right on to what has become the Forest Walk. After descending from the headland, the vegetation starts to change and you continue along into forested areas with the taller trees providing some shade. At the clearing, turn sharply to your right and back into the forest. There is a sign at the track head detailing the Headland Walk. Vegetation in this area takes the shape of dry rainforest and the bird calls are plentiful. Leaving the rainforest area, the walk continues to the junction with the Headland Walk. Turn left and at Diamond Head Access Road, turn right to return to the Diamond Head Campground.

Along the Way:

The rivers, beaches and forests of the Crowdy Bay National Park provided a home and food source for the Birpai people for around 6000 years. Today the park and all that lies within continue to be culturally significant.

North West

Little Bald Rock Walk

Taking in the Border link Trail toward the NSW-Qld Border, this walk climbs the spine of large granite rock known as Little Bald Rock. The views are breath taking, clearing the Queensland border toward the Girraween National Park. The climb up the spine of Little Bald Rock is very achievable and you are sure to encounter a few geckos and skinks sunning themselves on the impressive granite slab.

Description: Starting at the Bald Rock Campground and Picnic Area, take the signposted Border Link Trail in a southwest direction. The Little Bald Rock walk veers off to the left of the Border Link Trail and follows along the bottom of Bald Rock before climbing up the spine of the rock. The trail is marked and easily followed. The trail loops back down through the boulders to re-join the Border Link Trail.

Closest Town: Tenterfield

Start Location: Bald Rock Campground and Picnic Area, corner of Bald Rock Road and Bookookoorara Trail, Carrolls Creek. Travel 29 km north of Tenterfield on the sealed Woodenbong Road, turn onto the Bald Rock Road.

Latitude and longitude: 28.845512°S, 152.045847°E

Grade: 4

Trail Quality: Short steep climbs, some steps, formed track, some obstacles underfoot. Clearly signposted.

Distance: 7.5 km

Time: 3 hours 30 minutes

Amenities: Bush toilets at the campground at the start

Park Type: Bald Rock National Park

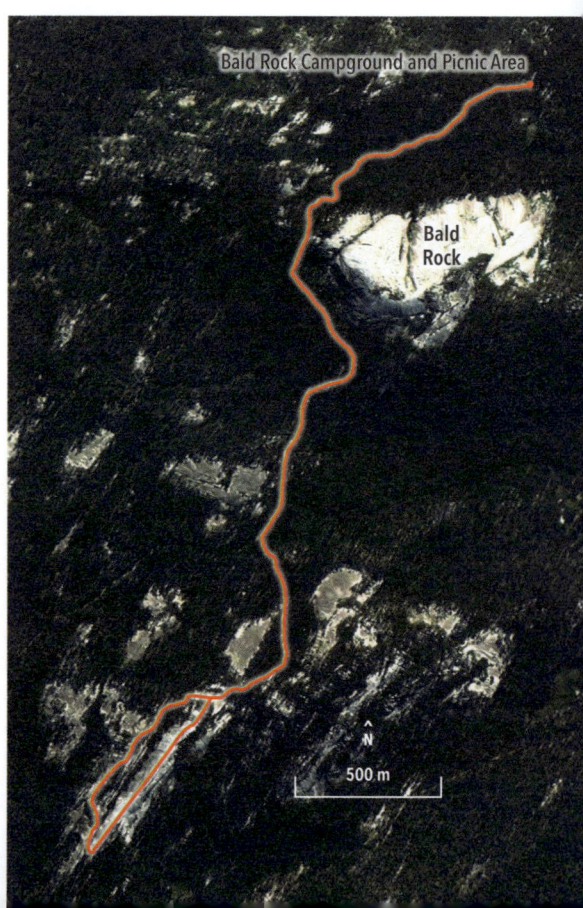

Bald Rock Campground and Picnic Area

Bald Rock

N

500 m

Along the Way:

Bald Rock is 750 metres long and 500 metres wide. It stands 1300 metres above sea level and creates an imposing impression on the surrounding landscape. The dome of Bald Rock is the largest granite formation in Australia.

Boronias and Banksias make their home in abundance in this area and are magnificent in spring.

If you find yourself on Bald Rock at dusk, notice the hue of the rockface changes colour from orange to yellow as the light changes.

The Kangaroos in the area are very curious and you may find some hopping along in the bushland as you travel the trails.

Bald Rock once served as a neutral territory and important trading place for the Aboriginal Nations of the Jukambal, Bundgalung and Kamillaroi people. Meeting on Bald Rock was able to occur without any nation travelling through other nations territory.

Bald Rock Summit Walk

The Bald Rock Summit track journeys through bushland teaming with wildlife and up to the summit of the largest granite rock in Australia, Bald Rock. With two routes to the summit, an adventurous walk awaits. The summit, standing 1300 metres above sea level offers vast views and the feeling of being on top of the world. A culturally significant site for three first nations peoples, the Jukambal, Bundgalung and Kamilleroi once used this imposing natural landmark as a neutral meeting and trading place. Views extend across the Queensland border into the Girraween National Park.

Description: Starting at the Bald Rock Picnic Area, there are two routes that can be taken to the summit.

Bungoona Walk

Grade: 3 **Distance:** 5 km **Time:** 2 hours
The Bungoona Walk is a gravel walking track. It winds up through the granite tors and large boulders to the summit.

Rockface Walk

Grade: 5 **Distance:** 1.6 km **Time:** 1 hour

The Rockface Walk lives up to its name and climbs up the steep side of Bald Rock. There are white markers which show the route to follow. This option should be considered carefully during rainy weather due to the slippery nature of the rocks.

Park Type: Bald Rock National Park

Along the Way:

Granite tors, initially formed underground as molten rock which eventually cooled, cracked and weathered into various smooth shapes are scattered around the landscape like discarded marbles. As the earth eroded away, the tors were exposed and further weathering by the wind, rain and sun, contributing to the unique shapes stacked neatly throughout the park.

Closest Town: Tenterfield

Start Location: Bald Rock Campground and Picnic Area, corner of Bald Rock Road and Bookookoorara Trail, Carrolls Creek. Travel 29 km north of Tenterfield on the sealed Woodenbong Road, turn onto the Bald Rock Road.

Latitude and longitude: 28.845512°S, 152.045847°E

Grade: 3

Trail Quality: Can be steep and slippery underfoot, some obstacles. Signposted.

Time: 2 hours

Amenities: Bush toilets at the campground at the start

Mystery Face Walking Track

Highlights of this walk are the remarkable granite rock formations. As you walk through the open woodland and imposing stands of granite boulders, let your imagination go wild as the rocks appear to take shape and resemble all manner of life. Toward the end of the walk, the granite boulder with the mystery face, of which the walk is named, will appear. It is not known if the Mystery Face boulder was formed by human hand or a freak of natural weathering.

Description: Upon making your way to the Mystery Face Picnic Ground, locate the information board which is at the start of the Mystery Face track head.

And along the way there is a diversion to Westminster Rocks which is worth the extra walk before continuing the route to the Mystery Face Rock.

The track is in a loop and signposted, easy to navigate and on formed trail.

Closest Town: Tenterfield

Start Location: Mystery Face picnic area. As you enter the Torrington State Conservation Area from Torrington, turn into Silent Grove Road. After 2.5 km, turn left onto Butlers Road and continue for 4.5 km to Mystery Face Road and then reach Mystery Face Picnic Area.

Latitude and longitude: 29.295909°S, 151.642408°E

Grade: 3

Trail Quality: A formed track, gentle hills, some obstacles, signposted.

Distance: 2.6 km

Time: 1 hours 30 minutes

Amenities: No

Park Type: Torrington State Conservation Area

Along the Way:

Mystery Face Rock is a large granite boulder with features not unlike a face. It is unknown who made the face in the boulder, whether it is a freak sculpture of natural creation or whether it was done by human hand. Either way, it is an intriguing sight.

Torrington State Conservation Area is home to a vast array of flora and fauna. There are 45 rare or threatened plant species including the Torrington Wattle and the Beadle's Grevillea and over 750 plant species in total, some of which only grow in the unique conditions of the conservation area. The fauna is equally as intriguing with Torrington SCA providing habitat to threatened species including the Tiger Quoll and the Powerful Owl and a further 20 mammal species, 135 different birds, 29 reptiles and 13 frog species.

Mystery Face
picnic area

Mystery Face Rd

N

100 m

Murrumbooee Cascades Trail

Plunging over the edge of the escarpment, waters of the Murrumbooee Cascades create a spectacular sight. Along the way you pass through thick rainforest and tall eucalypts before dropping down to a networks of creeks and waterways with many spectacular water features through the granite boulders and slabs. The walk uphill out of the creek area is a challenge however the rewards of the untouched waters of the Gibraltar National Park and the Murrumbooee Cascades make it all worthwhile.

Description: From Mulligans Hut, the initial part of the walk is along pleasantly wide and groomed trail through tall eucalypt forest. Shortly after starting there is a side trip to the Barra Nulla Cascades. This is

Closest Town: Glen Innes

Start Location: Mulligans Hut, Mulligans Flat Trail off Mulligans Drive, Gibraltar Range

Latitude and longitude: 29.516108°S, 152.360973°E

Grade: 4

Trail Quality: Formed track, steep in places. Clearly signposted.

Distance: 6 km

Time: 2 hours 30 minutes

Amenities: Yes

Park Type: Gibraltar Range National Park

signposted and just 20 metres each way, so well worth the time. The landscape starts to change and you find yourself in lush green rainforest with the trail covered in leaf litter. The ferns, vines and moss become more prolific the further you walk.

The next junction you come to is the signposted junction for the Forest Walk on your left which leads down to the granite tors of Lyrebird Rock and Murrumbooee Cascades. Continue straight to Murrumbooee Cascades.

You will cross a small bridge on the track before starting to descend into the creek valley. The descent is steep and the trail narrows. However once at Little Dandahra Creek the trail gently meanders along. There are various creek crossings and water features along the way and the track continues to the Weir which also serves as a great swimming hole, picnic spot and the turnaround point.

Retrace your steps to return to the start.

Along the way:

Mulligans Hut is the site of the ambitious project of entrepreneur Mr Bill Mulligan who proposed a hydroelectric scheme in the 1920s. The project never came to fruition and all that remains is a hut and two weirs. The first weir is at the campground and the second is at the end of the Murrumbooee Cascades track.

The Gibraltar Range National Park provides sanctuary and habitat to the endangered giant barred frog. A dark olive-green colour, the giant barred frog can grow to over 11 centimetres and makes its home amongst flowing streams in rainforest or wet sclerophyll environments.

Tommy's Rock Lookout Walk

Named after local aboriginal bushranger Tommy McPherson, Tommy's Rock, an impressive rocky outcrop, stands 1013 metres above sea level. Due to its views of the vast landscape below, the eponymous Tommy reputedly used as Tommy's Lookout for his more questionable pursuits.

The eastern border of the reserve – where the Old Grafton Road runs – was the thoroughfare for the weekly Cobb and Co mail run, and the main route into and out of the area for locally mined gold. This made Tommy's Rock a great vantage point from which to plan his bushranging activities.

In recent times, Tommy's Rock has become a coveted destination for walkers. Rated at grade 5, the trail is challenging, steep and rewarding.

The reserve also serves as a haven for over 50 species of protected birdlife. It is not uncommon to see yellow-rumped thornbills, yellow faced honeyeaters, and the majestic king parrot. Flora of the area is diverse and the view from Tommy's Rock is magnificent.

Closest Town: Glen Innes

Start Location: Narrow Pass Trail, Diehard 2370. Turn off the Gwydir Highway at Glen Elgin into Old Grafton Road. Drive 16.8 km, passing the Mann River Campground, then turn into Narrow Pass Trail and park at the entrance to Mann River Nature Reserve. From here it is a 4.5 kilometre climb up the Narrow Pass Trail to the summit.

Latitude and longitude: 29.716477°S, 152.099192°E

Grade: 5

Trail Quality: Formed track, rough, steep, some obstacles, no signage along the way.

Distance: 9 km return

Time: 3 hours 30 minutes

Amenities: none

Park Type: Mann River Nature Reserve

Description: Starting at the track head of the Narrow Pass Trail, follow the main vehicle track uphill and away from the track head. The track itself is not at all picturesque, however keep a lookout for over 50 different species of protected birdlife that make their home in the Mann River Nature Reserve.

As you gain elevation, the roar of the Mann River will be heard some 400m below and as you reach the summit, full views of the river come into sight as it winds its way along

the base of the Great Dividing Range in the valley below.

There are two minor junctions where other tracks enter the Narrow Pass Trail on the way to the summit, stay to the right-hand option at each junction. Return via the same route, taking care to stay left on the way down.

Along the Way:

Birdlife: over 50 species of birds are protected in the reserve. Bring binoculars if birds are your thing. A sighting of the regal Peregrine Falcon is also possible if you keep your eyes peeled skyward where the mountain thermals blow.

Native mammals are plentiful including the Pretty-Faced Wallabies, Brush-Tailed Rock Wallabies and Wallaroos.

Lace Monitors are also known to inhabit the area, some reaching lengths of 2 metres.

Tommys Rock Lookout

Narrow Pass Trail

Old Grafton Rd

600 m

Washpool Walk

A well signposted walk through the warm temperate forests of the Washpool National Park, this loop walk showcases the best of the pristine and timeless Gondwana Rainforest. Highlights on this walk include one of the largest stands of Coachwood Trees in New South Wales, multiple waterfalls, Cedar Trees over 1000 years old and some impressive strangler figs. Birdlife is abundant and the rich soils of this ancient rainforest host a myriad of flora and fauna.

Description: Starting at the signposted track head in Coombadjha campground, the walk begins by following the creek, then slowly makes its way uphill. From the top of the hill, continue along the management track and re-enter the forest. Signs indicate the way down to Summit Falls which is a short detour off the main track and quite worthwhile. Hakea Trail will come in from the right not long after returning from Summit Falls. Continue along the main trail, cross Cedar Creek and the trail shortly after follows Coombadjha Creek back to the campground. The walk is straight forward and signposted.

Coombadjha campground

Coachwood Dr.

Along the Way:

Satin Bower Birds, Bell Birds and the ever-industrious Lyrebird are commonly spotted. Rare birds including the Rufous Scrub bird and the Powerful Owl also make their home in Washpool National Park.

Washpool National Park was established in 1983. Prior to National Park status, selective logging in the area saw many red cedar trees harvested. The local logging history dates back to the early 1800s and the days of bullock teams and crosscut saws.

It is recommended that you might like to take swimmers if the weather is warm as there is a great swimming area along the creek which is signposted.

Closest Town: Glen Innes

Start Location: Coombadjha campground, end of Coachwood Drive, Gibraltar Range, Washpool National Park. 76 km from Glen Innes via the Gwydir Hwy.

Latitude and longitude: 29.471548°S, 152.321232°E

Grade: 4

Trail Quality: Some short and steep hills, many steps, rough track with obstacles under foot. Clearly signposted.

Distance: 8.3 km

Time: 3 hours 30 minutes

Amenities: Yes, bush toilets at the start

Park Type: Washpool National Park

Wollomombi Walking Track and the Chandler Walk

Taking in the outer rim of the Wollomombi Gorge rewards walkers with some amazing views of the Wollomombi Falls and Chandler Falls. This walk takes in Eagle Lookout, Wollomombi Falls Lookout and the famed Chandler Falls Lookout. Following the Wollomombi Walking Track, the walk continues and takes in the Main Lookout and the Checks Viewpoint. Each give different vantage points from which to observe the wild Wollomombi Gorge and the rivers that have calved a path through.

Description: From Wollomombi Falls Picnic Area, follow the relatively easy trail for 700 metres to Eagle Lookout. Eagle Lookout is a teaser lookout – you can look into the gorge, you can hear the waterfalls, but you cannot see any waterfalls from this point.

Continue from Eagle Lookout along the trail and approximately 500 metres further you will cross a bridge over the Wollomombi River. There is a steep climb out from the river basin and 400 metres on you reach the Wollomombi Falls Lookout.

From Wollomombi Falls Lookout, you get as close as you will to the Falls but you only see part pf the waterfall. The thundering sounds of the falls after rain, coupled with the fine water spray adds to the atmosphere of the gorge.

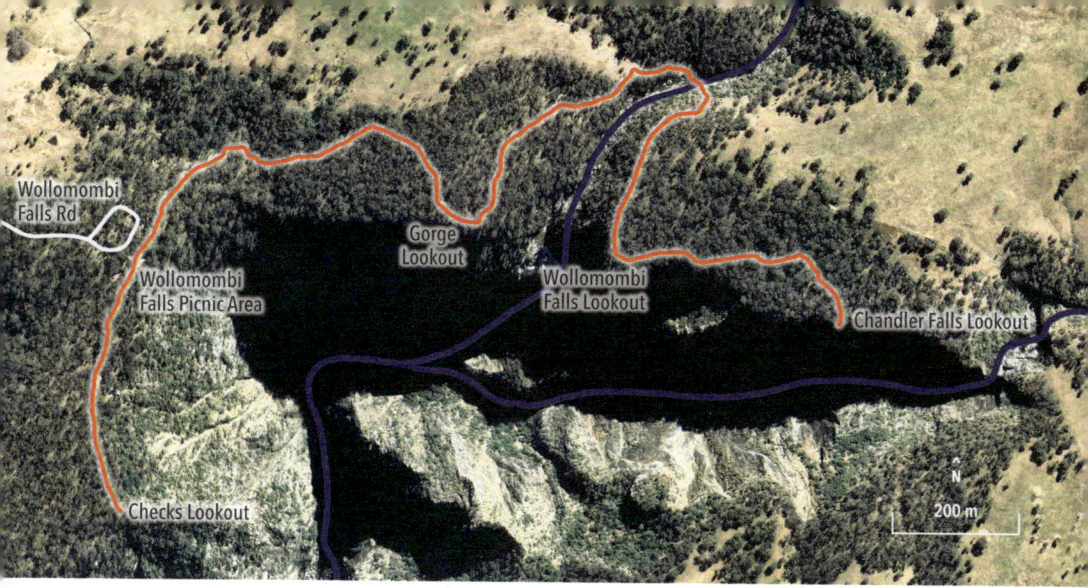

500 metres further along the trail is Chandler Falls Lookout, the final lookout on the route. This lookout reveals the entire waterfall and the vast drop to the bottom of the gorge.

Retrace your steps back to the Wollomombi Falls Picnic area and follow the signs to the Chandler Walk. 200 metres into the Chandler Walk is the Main Lookout. This lookout gives you a direct view of both Chandler Falls and Wollomombi Falls. You get a full grasp of the scale of the Wollomombi Gorge from this vantage point.

Continue along for 300 metres to the Checks Viewpoint which offers a more focused view of the gorge. While the Chandler Walk continues, it does not offer anything of further value to the experience. Retrace your steps back to the Wollomombi Picnic Area where there are barbeque and picnic facilities.

Closest Town: Armidale

Start Location: Wollomombi Falls Picnic Area. Turn off the Waterfall Way into Wollomombi Falls Road at Hillgrove and drive south for 1.7 km to the picnic area.

Latitude and longitude: 30.531892°S, 152.033460°E

Grade: 3

Trail Quality: Formed Track, some steps, undulating with a short steep section near the river. Some obstacles underfoot. Clearly signposted.

Distance: 5.1 km

Time: 3 hours

Amenities: Yes, at the picnic area

Park Type: Oxley Wild Rivers National Park

Along the Way:

Water takes 22 seconds to fall the 260 metres from the top to the bottom of the Falls.

Wollomombi River crossing is an opportunity to peer into the waterway looking for Platypus which are known to frequent the area.

Wedge-Tailed Eagles appear to enjoy the thermals that rise out of the Wollomombi Gorge and can often be seen effortlessly hovering above.

Chandler Falls lookout has an amazing viewing platform looking down into the Wollomombi Gorge and across to the Wollomombi Falls and Chandler Falls.

Yulludunida Walking Track

Rising 350 metres in just 1.5 km, the Yulludunida Walking Track is a challenging undertaking with a rewarding view of the mountain crater and across the Mount Kaputar National Park at the summit.

Description: Leaving Green Camp, this is a challenging walk from the outset. The track climbs up through a gully before breaking out from the tree cover and following close to the escarpment. While the track is formed, the country is steep, and you may need to stop and take in the views regularly. When you reach the dingo proof fence, the trail ceases and the rest of the way to the summit of the bluff is a rock scramble. The views at the top are vast and look over the northwest of New South Wales and the Mount Kaputar National Park. Retrace your steps back to Green Camp carpark.

Closest Town: Narrabri

Start Location: Green Camp, Kaputar Road, Kaputar. Green Camp is about 38 km from Narrabri. From town, drive south east along Old Gunnedah Rd, then turn left into Kaputar Road.

Latitude and longitude: 30.279031°S, 150.083969°E

Grade: 4

Trail Quality: Steep, many steps, some obstacles underfoot. Limited trail markings. Unformed trail with rock hopping in the upper section of the walk.

Distance: 3 km

Time: 2 hours

Amenities: none

Park Type: Mount Kaputar National Park

Along the Way:

Reptile life is plentiful in the area, especially in the high parts of the walk. This can entice birds of prey, be sure to look skyward for wedge-tailed eagles soaring.

Home to the Gamilaroi Aboriginal people, resources were plentiful including food, traditional medicines and shelters. Rock carvings, marks on trees and grinding groves in the rocks are relics from aboriginal life on the land.

The brightly coloured Mount Kaputar Pink Slug, a species of giant air-breathing land slug, is found plentifully in the Mt Kaputar National Park after rain. Keep a lookout among rocks, branches and throughout the ground coverings for this bright pink local.

Green Camp

Kaputar Rd

Mt Yulludunida

N

100 m

West and Outback

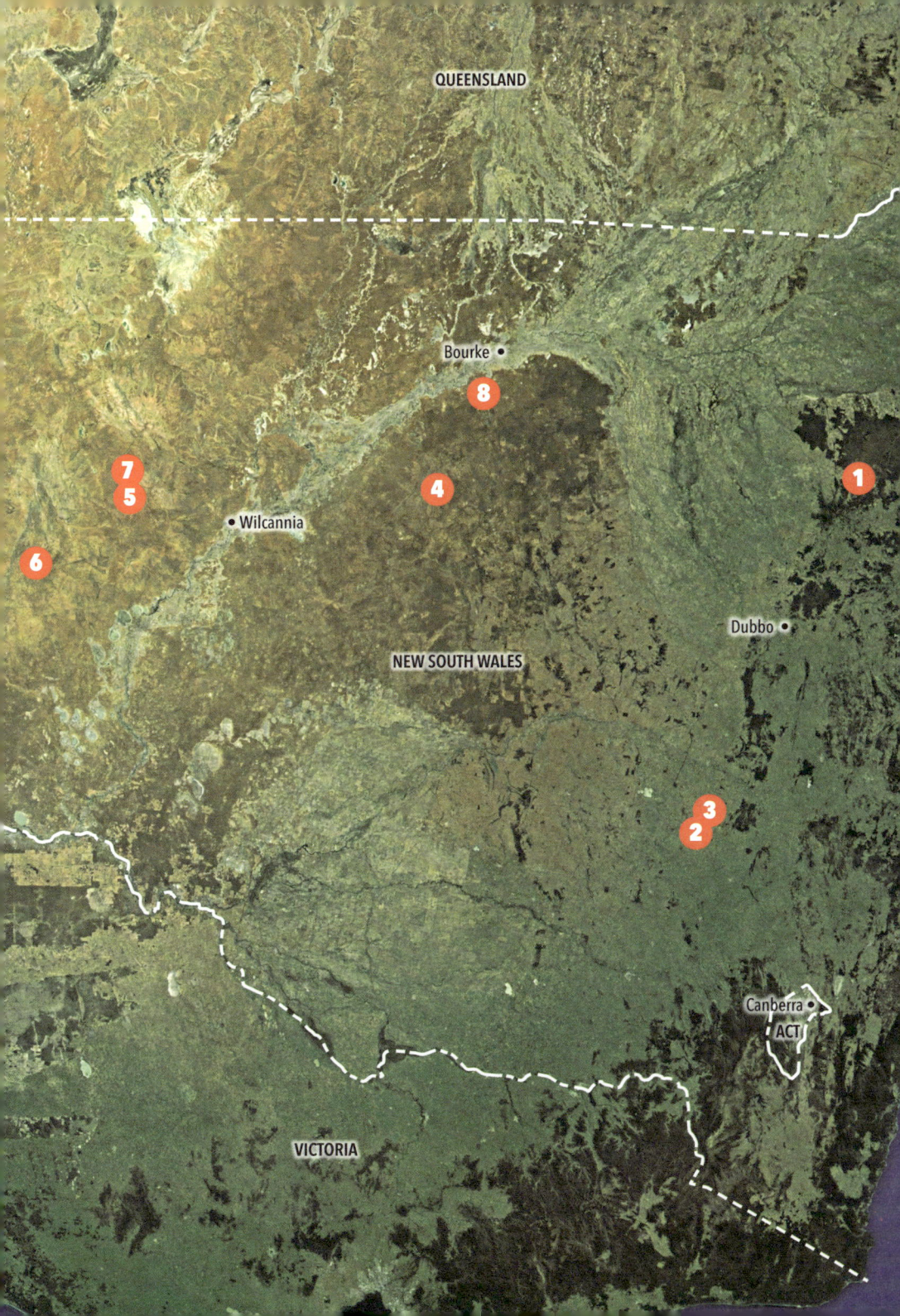

Sculpture in the Scrub

In the unique forests of the Piliga, the Timmallallie National Park hosts the award winning 'Sculptures in the Scrub'. Five renowned sculpture artists were commissioned to enhance the natural beauty of the Dandry Gorge and provide an ongoing record of the site's significance to its early Aboriginal occupants. Over a period of 4 years, they collaborated with local Gamilaroi Elders to create sculptures that reflected the cultural beliefs and stories of the local Gamilaroi people. This walk is intriguing and informative.

Description: Starting at the Sculptures in the Scrub picnic area, the walk is sign posted and includes information boards at each of the five sculptures sites along the way.

You can extend this walk by waking down into Dandry Gorge and along the dry creek bed, where the towering gorge walls cast shadows. The extension is a 3 kilometre loop which begins just past the last sculpture. It is much more rugged underfoot than the Sculptures in the Scrub Walk.

Closest Town: Baradine and Coonabarabran

Start Location: Sculptures in the Scrub picnic area, end of Dandry Gorge Road, Baradine. Inside Timmallallie National Park.

Latitude and longitude: 30.996780°S, 149.234554°E

Grade: 3

Trail Quality: Formed trail, gentle hills and some steps. Signposted and easy to follow.

Distance: 2.4 km

Time: 2 hours

Amenities: Yes, at the start

Park Type: Timmallallie National Park

The route is signposted at the end of the Sculptures in the Scrub walk. It is recommended to take extra gear for safety including water, jacket and food with you if entering the gorge.

Along the Way:

There are five sculpture sites. Each site features the sculpture, an information board which details the artist who created the piece, a little about the process of creating the sculpture and the deeper meaning of the sculpture to the Gamillaroi People.

Artist Ken Hutchinson created *Yundu Yundu*, one sculpture in white marble and the other in dark grey granite. These sculptures represented Aboriginal tools and both were enticing to touch, both reflecting the temperatures of the environment differently.

Badger Bates' rock carving collaboration *Connections* is earthly in its presentation and pays homage to the connection between myth and science.

Col Henry's piece, entitled *Scrub Spirit* has two elements and is created in stainless steel. The material sits in stark contrast against the natural Piliga forest. This piece shows a combination of throwing sticks and two slim figures looking out over the valley.

Brett Garing's *First Lesson* is a true masterpiece, cast in bronze. First Lesson invokes a strong sense of the relationship of the aboriginal people with their children and the passing of knowledge through the generations.

Respect Mother, a series of mosaic sculptures by Pamela Denise – reflects the women of the Piliga and how they have and continue to use the resources of the land.

There are barbeques and picnic facilities at the picnic area making it a great place to spend the day.

Timmallallie National Park

200 m

Sculptures in the Scrub picnic area

Bertha's Gully Walking Track and Ben Halls Cave

Named after Bertha Seaton from the historic Seaton's Farm, Bertha's Gully Walking Track journeys up through Bertha's Gully to the sublime Bertha's Gully waterfall, a secluded and idyllic place. Bertha Seaton and her husband Jim had worked the Seaton family farm, a 150-acre allotment from the time of the depression until 1983 when Jim died. The farm is still as it was left when Bertha moved off the land to Grenfell and sold the property to the National Parks and Wildlife Service. On the way back from Bertha's Gully Waterfalls a small detour takes you past Ben Halls Cave, a place he sought refuge between bush ranging activities.

Closest Town: Grenfell

Start Location: Ben Halls Camping Area, Piney Range. From the Mid-Western Highway at Grenfell, turn into Back Piney Ridge Road and head west. Eventually the road swings south and becomes Nowlans Road. As you pass the park entrance, turn left (east) and continue 4 km to your destination.

Latitude and longitude: 33.906741°S, 147.950414°E

Grade: 4

Trail Quality: Rough under foot, many obstacles and steps. Limited signage.

Distance: 4.3 km

Time: 3 hours

Amenities: Yes, at the camping area

Park Type: Weddin Mountains National Park

Description: Bertha's Gully Walking Track starts opposite the barbeque area at Ben Halls Camping Area. Walk toward the Ben Halls Cave Walking Track. Cross the ford and continue on until you reach the turn to the left for Ben Halls Cave, then continue straight, staying on your current route. Further along you will pass another turn to Ben Halls Cave, again continue along your current route. The route swings around to your left and begins to ascend into the gully. The rock faces on each side rise up around you, giving clear direction to your path.

The rocky overhangs and forested area are enchanting as you make your way steadily up the incline to Bertha's Gully Waterfall. You will make your

second water crossing just prior to arriving at the falls.

Returning the way you came, as you reach the turn to Ben Halls Cave – turn right and follow this track as it loops past Ben Halls Cave and back onto Bertha's Gully Walking Track. The loop is under 1 kilometre long and as you come to Bertha's Gully Walking Track you turn right and make your way back to Ben Halls Camping Area.

Along the Way:

Ben Halls Cave offers perfect panoramic views across the surrounding farmland, giving ample time for Mr Hall and his cohorts to go into hiding if they spotted approaching lawmen.

If you are interested in knowing more about Bertha Seaton and her life in the Weddin Mountains area, you can visit **Seaton's Farm Historic Site** which is a short walk from Ben Halls Camping Area.

Seaton's farm was purchased at the height of the depression and sits peacefully at the base of Bertha's Gully. Today the farm buildings and machinery are as they were left and demonstrate how resourceful the Seaton's were. With little money to their name, the Seaton's used second

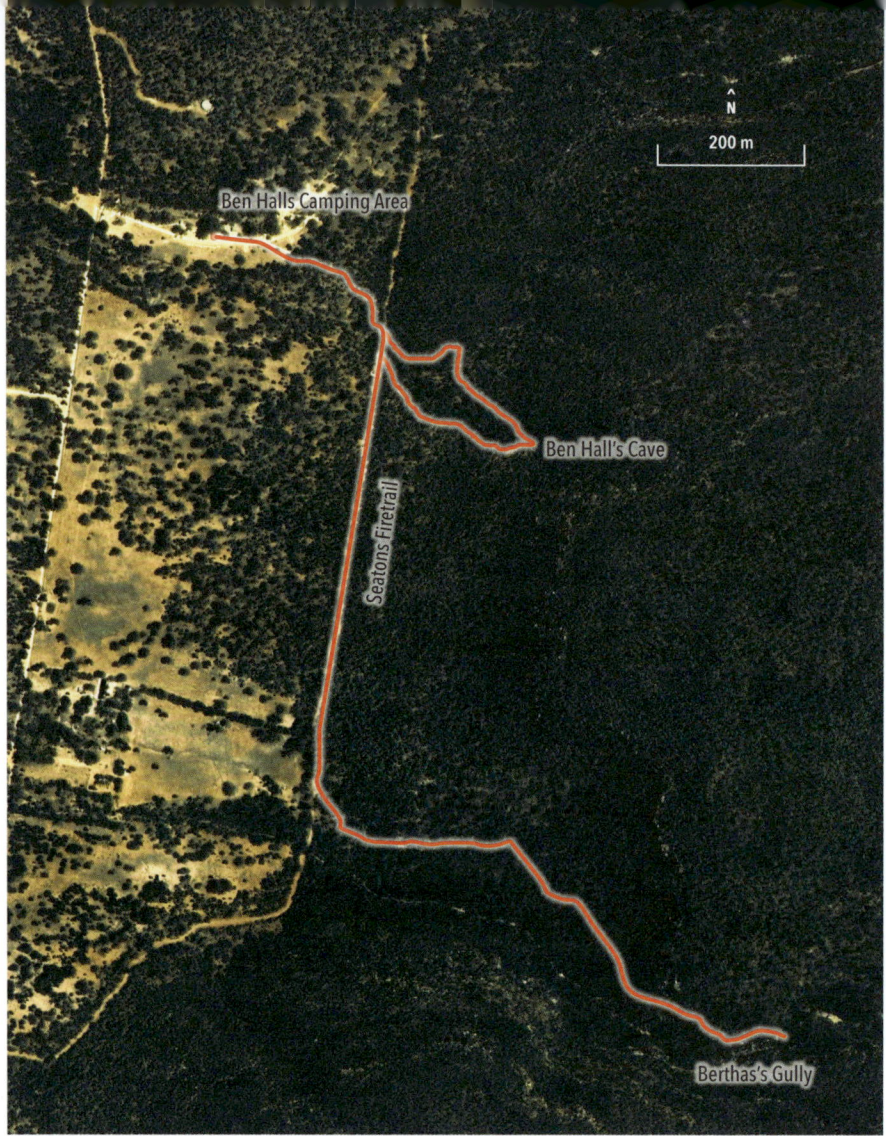

hand building supplies and offcuts to make what was their home. Forging out a working farm on marginal land, their ingenuity and determination can be seen in the relics that remain.

Seaton's Farm is well signposted with information boards.

Spring is a divine time in the Weddin Mountains National Park, Wildflowers are in full bloom and lilies and orchids sprout abundantly. The diversity in the vegetation in this area, provides ample nourishment for a large range of birdlife and wildlife.

Eualdrie Walking Track

From the remote Holy Camp area, this walk takes in the Peregrine Lookout and the Eualdrie lookout. Peregrine Lookout gives you views over the township of Grenfell and Eualdrie Lookout pleases with panoramic views over sandstone escarpments, farming landscape and the picturesque and rugged Weddin Mountains. A famed hideout for bushrangers in the mid 1800s, Ben Hall is rumoured to have hidden at least some of the loot from the famous Escort Rock Gold Robbery in Eugowra in 1862 in the area. It has never been found.

Description: From Holy Camp, follow the old logging track as it climbs steeply from the campground and makes its way up the mountain to Peregrine Lookout. The views here stretch all the way to Grenfell and the outlying farmland that surrounds it. Continue onwards and as you gain altitude, the track winds through health and diverse woodlands. Glimpses of sandstone escarpments and tended farmland can be seen periodically through the tree line.

After 2.3 km, there is a turn to your right to Eualdrie Lookout. The track to the lookout is another 80 metres onwards. Eualdrie Lookout offers views across the Weddin mountain range with a vast look at all the National Park has to offer.

Returning from the lookout, after 80 metres, turn left onto Eualdrie Lookout Track at the junction and continue back along the route, predominantly downhill for 2.3 km to Holy Camp Area.

Along the Way:

In the mid 1800s, the Weddin mountain range was a hideout for notorious bushranger Ben Hall and his accomplice John Bow. Both men,

Closest Town: Grenfell

Start Location: Holy Camp. From Mary Gilmore Way, turn west onto Holy Camp Road, after 14 km you come to Holy Camp.

Latitude and longitude: 33.898017°S, 148.003070°E

Grade: 4

Trail Quality: Rough Track, many obstacles under foot, occasional steps, limited signage.

Distance: 4.8 km

Time: 3 hours 15 minutes

Amenities: Yes, At Holy Camp.

Park Type: Weddin Mountains National Park

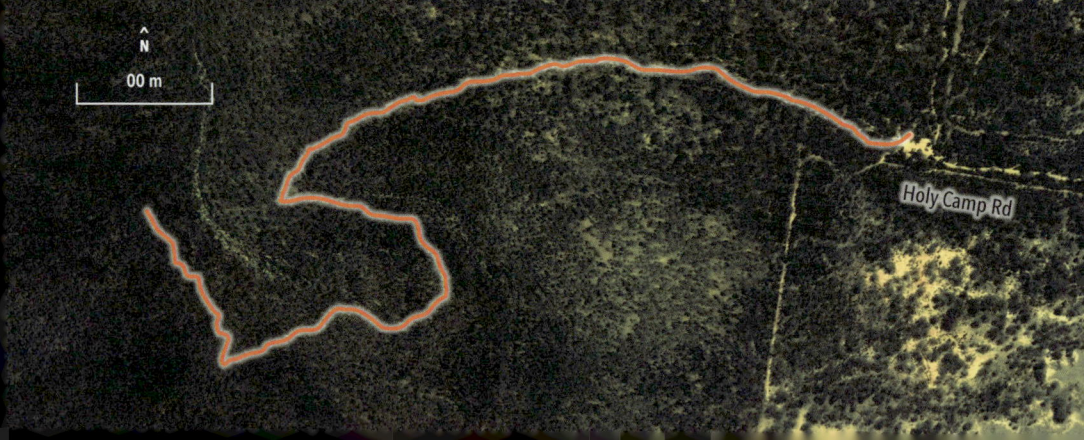

wanted for their involvement in the Escort Robbery some 70 km away near Eugowra, sought refuge in the rugged landscapes of the Weddin Mountain Range.

12 threatened plant species and 39 threatened bird species make the Weddin mountain national park their safe haven.

'Weddin' comes from the Wiradjuri word 'Weedin', meaning place to sit, stay or remain. The Weddin Mountains were a traditional ceremonial site where aboriginal youth were initiated with a period of enforced isolation.

The birdlife in the National park is diverse and includes emu's, peregrine falcons, wedge-tailed eagles, robins and thornbills making it an exciting birdwatching experience.

N

00 m

Holy Camp Rd

Ngiyampaa Walkabout Track

Returned to the traditional owners in 2004, the Mount Grenfell Historic Site protects some of the most impressive and expressive aboriginal art sites in New South Wales. This track is steeped in Aboriginal History. The trail leads past the art sites to Mount Grenfell and the Choy Trig Marker where you can look out over the vast arid landscapes of the outback.

Description: After parking, walk along the old access road for approximately 200metres and through the old carpark to the track head. The initial part of the route makes its way to the various art sites along a paved stone track. It is well signposted in this area, and easy to follow. As you reach the sandy creek the art is on the low overhangs along the creek. While the overhangs have been fenced off for preservation, they are still easily viewed and photographed.

Closest Town: Cobar

Start Location: Mount Grenfell Art Site carpark, Mount Grenfell Historic Site. 73 km from Cobar via Pupulla Road. The site is 1 km east of the intersection of Pupulla Road and Mount Grenfell Trail, Cubba.

Latitude and longitude: 31.302115°S, 145.306339°E

Grade: 4

Trail Quality: Initially smooth trail as far as the art sites, then the trail is rough underfoot with loose rocks along the track. Inclines are not too onerous. Well signposted and marked.

Distance: 4.9 km

Time: 2 hours

Amenities: none

Park Type: Mount Grenfell Historic Site

After spending some time at the art sites, continue along the Ngiyampaa Walkabout Track as climbs gently through wooded and grassy areas and makes its way around the catchment of the creek. The trail changes after the art sites and in places the footpad can become faint however there are continual markers to keep you on the right route. Once on the ridge line, the track makes its way to the Choy trig marker on Mount Grenfell and the vast views across the sunburned arid plains below. With little by way of intriguing land formations, the remnants of long forgotten gold mines appear to be the only defining marks on the landscape. Descending from the Choy trig marker down to

the creek, the trail is rocky and loose underfoot at times. Follow the trail back to the old carpark and further along to the start.

Along the Way:

Trig stations were instrumental in the process of triangulation for the purpose of mapping by early settlers. 'Trig' is short for the word 'trigonometric'.

Wildlife in the Mount Grenfell Historic Site is plentiful, all types of reptile life are active on hotter days and Emu, Kangaroo's and wallabies are all happily at home in the area.

Mixed breed foraging flocks, usually inhabiting areas of high resources, inhabit the area and you may see red-capped robins and birds of similar size such as thornbills all foraging together. It is thought the mixed breed flocks are bought together to reduce a predators ability to single out one prey and increase the birds ability to spot prey.

The waterhole on Mount Grenfell was an important place for generations of the Ngiyampaa Aboriginal people. The Ngiyampaa people are dry land people from the regions of the arid plains and rocky hill country.

During the early 1900s, European settlers dislodged the Ngiyampaa people and many were relocated to the Murrin Bridge area. The Ngiyampaa people maintain strong connections with the land of the area and in 2004, Mount Grenfell Historical Site was handed back to the traditional owners.

N

400 m

Mount Grenfell
Historical Site

Homestead Gorge Walking Track

The red cliffs of Homestead Gorge are home to some ancient aboriginal rock engravings as well as much needed respite in the harsh outback climate. Wallabies, goannas and emu dot the countryside enroute to the gorge and the arid landscape reveals little about the beauty of the gorge until it reveals itself.

Description: The track starts at the northern end of the campground. Along the way you will find interpretive signage with information on the history, culture, fauna and flora of the area. There are also directional confidence markers to guide your way. The directional markers you need to follow are marked red.

Closest Town: Broken Hill

Start Location: Homestead Creek picnic area, Mutawintji Rd, Mutawintji. As you enter Mutawintji National Park, continue past the visitor's centre for approximately 2 km. Homestead Creek picnic area is on your right. It is about 130 km from Broken Hill via the Silver City Highway.

Latitude and longitude: 31.282406°S, 142.295259°E

Grade: 5

Trail Quality: rough unformed track, mostly flat, some obstacles underfoot. Minimal directional markings.

Distance: 7.5 km

Time: 3 hours 45 minutes

Amenities: At the Homestead Creek Campground

Park Type: Mutawintji National Park

As you set out, the track travels parallel with the dry riverbed. Passing the picnic area, you enter the gorge area. The landscape changes are apparent you soon reach the Aboriginal Rock Art Gallery. There is a viewing platform with interpretive signs that detail what you are looking at. From here the trail drops down into the creek bed and through the natural gorge with the trail following the natural flow of the landscape there are several creek crossings along the way.

Further along the gorge, you pass the junction to Rockholes Loop Walking Track. At the junction there is also some

rock art to view. The Homestead Gorge Walking Track continues straight following the gorge. There are directional confidence markers (red) which lead the way. As you travel along the gorge, the landscape will split, you need to take the left side option. A few hundred metres later you come to the end of the gorge and the coveted waterhole. If the weather is hot, the water, which is usually cold, is great respite before making the return trip. Directional markers assist you to retract your steps back to Homestead Creek Campground.

Along the Way:

The Gorge is the champion of the walk. From the dull arid landscapes prior to the gorge, the red cliffs give shelter to aboriginal rock engravings and are a haven in a harsh climate.

Depending upon the time of day and the heat, you may see wallabies, goannas or emu on your trip.

A significant meeting place for the Malyankapa and Pandijikali Aboriginal people, at times up to 1000 people would come together for initiations, rainmaking and other ceremonies. Information boards detail aboriginal activity in the area.

Living Desert, The Sculptures Walk and Sanctuary Walk

The Sculptures Walk observes the work of world-renowned sculptors and the result of their artistic toiling through 53 tonnes of sandstone. The Sanctuary Cultural Walk in the John Simons flora and fauna sanctuary explores the Natural and Cultural Heritage of the area.

Closest Town: Broken Hill

Amenities: Yes

Start Location: Sanctuary Cultural Walk car park, Living Desert State Park, Broken Hill. 12 km north of Broken Hill via Nine Mile Road.

Latitude and longitude: 31.892541°S, 141.453429°E

The Sculpture Walk

In just 6 weeks, a team of 12 sculptors transformed sandstone rock which had been transported in from Wilcannia in the east to the Sundown area, into 12 impressive Sculptures designed to reflect and enhance the natural light and capture the imagination.

Description: The Sculpture Walk is well sign posted with information and directions at every stop. The walk includes 12 sculptures each with their own story to tell. With titles such as 'Motherhood' and 'The Bride' and 'Angels of the Sun and Moon' time will pass by quickly as you learn about the stories behind the sculpture.

Grade: 2

Distance: 2.6 km

Time: 2 hours

Park Type: Living Desert State Park

Sanctuary Cultural Walk Trails

Bordered by predator proof fencing, the John Simons Flora and Fauna sanctuary, 180 hectares, gives protection a diverse range of Flora and Fauna. Wallaroos and Red Kangaroos are plentiful and wander freely under the protection of the sanctuary.

Grade: 2
Distance: 2.2 km
Time: 1 hour 30 minutes

Description: The walk has many stops with information boards and directional signage guiding the experience of both cultural, historical and natural significance. The wildflowers are plentiful, there is an arboretum to visit, scenic lookouts, quartz outcrops, geological information and interpretation and an animal viewing hide. If history is more relevant to your visit there is a prospector mine site to visit.

Trail Quality: Easily followed and formed track.

Information boards are plentiful in the park to ensure you do not miss any of the many available experiences.

It is recommended to check with the Visitor Information Centre prior to travelling to the Living Desert State Park. Open and closing times differ throughout the seasons. An entry fee may apply.

Visitor Information Centre – Phone: (08) 8080 3560.

Mutawintji Gorge Walking Track

The Mutawintji Gorge Walking Track makes its way through the spectacular spacious and peaceful outback country of the Mutawintji National Park and to a peaceful waterhole surrounded by shape red cliffs. With Average summer temperatures above 30 degrees Celsius and highest temperatures well above 40 degrees, it is best to walk in the Mutawintji National Park in Spring, Winter or Autumn.

Description: From the track head, the trail immediately crosses the Old Mutawintji Creek, now a dry sandy creek bed, before heading in a south-eastern direction. The trail rises as it crosses a small hill and then picks up and then again follows the creek bed. As you follow the trail along, there are white confidence markers along the way and although there is no other signage, the trail is well defined in the landscape. As the gorge gets closer, the trail can at times be vague and harder to follow, and the landscape becomes more rugged.

The trail makes its way back alongside the creek bed and the

Closest Town: Broken Hill, 2880

Start Location: Mutawintji Gorge walking track is in the southern part of Mutawintji National Park. Parking is available at the Mutawintji Gorge Walking Track Head, at the end of Mutawintji Gorge Road, Mutawintji. Stop at the visitor centre for a map and advice on the latest conditions. It is about 132 km from Broken Hill via the Silver City Highway.

Latitude and longitude: 31.304402°S, 142.310360°E

Grade: 5

Trail Quality: Rough track, mostly unformed, some steps. Steep and difficult. White directional markers throughout the walk however limited signage.

Distance: 6 km

Time: 3 hours

Amenities: Yes, At the Visitors Centre

Park Type: Mutawintji National Park

countryside around the creek starts to close in with red rocks rising from the landscape encasing the creek bed into a valley of sorts. The creek bed ends abruptly, and the next part of the walk is over rocks and into the gorge. Although daunting, the rock scrambles protect a destination worthy of the effort. At the end of the gorge, the waterhole is surrounded by tall red rock cliffs which contrast brilliantly against the blue sky.

Return the way you came to the carpark. The visitors centre has shade and amenities.

Along the Way:

Mutawintji National Park is the home to the only colony of Yellow-footed rock wallabies in New South Wales. The Yellow-footed Rock Wallaby is an endangered species.

Feral Goats are plentiful in these parts and are responsible for some of the erosion in the semi-arid areas of the park.

There is an abundance of birdlife along the walk including: zebra finches, short-billed corella's, budgerigars and apostlebirds. Look skyward for sightings of Wedge-tailed eagles or peregrine falcons.

Little Mountain Walking Track

Rising up from the red soil and mulga woodlands of the Gundabooka National Park, the Gundabooka Range offers a unique walking experience with a rich history. Significant to the Ngemba and Kurnu Baakandji Aboriginal people, their long existence on the land is evidenced by rock art and markings in the area. In addition to being a place of ceremony, the Gundabooka Range served as a vital resource in times of low rainfall, with the creeks within the range offering water even during droughts. Little Mountain Walking Track offers a glimpse into the ruggedly beautiful outback National Park, and the summit of Mount Gundabooka shows off some amazing views northward across the range and plains.

Description: Leaving Dry Tank Campground southbound, the trail is well defined and easily followed. Meandering along the red dirt pathway, you

Closest Town: Bourke

Start Location: Dry Tank Campground and Picnic Area, Dry Tank Trail, 21 km west of the intersection of the Ben Lomond Road and Kidman Way, Gunderbooka. Carparking and the trail head is roughly 100 metres to the south of the campground.

Latitude and longitude: 30.518173°S, 145.714635°E

Grade: 4

Trail Quality: Gentle hills, occasional steps, formed track , some obstacles. Limited signage.

Distance: 4.8 km

Time: 3 hours

Amenities: Yes, at the start

Park Type: Gundabooka National Park and State Conservation Area

travel through low woodlands and scrubby bush, crossing a small steel bridge that appears to give passage over a very small gully. Continue on and the trail becomes a series of carefully placed rock pavers. The trail gentle steps upwards as you make your way through further open woodland and eventually to a small section of dirt path before the viewing platform appears.

Retrace your steps to return to the finish.

Along the Way:

There are information boards along the way detailing the Fauna and Flora of the area. Fauna is plentiful along the track, with Red Kangaroos, Emu and reptiles all a feature. Threatened bird species include the little pied bat, pink cockatoo and painted honeyeater.

The viewing platform offers unobscured views of the northern escarpment of the glorious Gunderbooka Range. Watching a sunset in the area is a sublime experience.

Spending a century as pastoral land, the stations of Ben Lomond, Belah and Mulgowan now make up the Gundabooka National Park. Homesteads, workers quarters, tanks, sheds and yards are still intact in the area and can be accessed by the public.

Index

First published in 2022 by New Holland Publishers
Sydney

Level 1, 178 Fox Valley Road, Wahroonga, NSW 2076, Australia

newhollandpublishers.com

A record of this book is held at the National Library of Australia.

ISBN 9781760795054

Group Managing Director: Fiona Schultz
Project Editor: Xavier Waterkeyn
Maps and design: Andrew Davies
Production Director: Arlene Gippert
Printed in China

10 9 8 7 6 5 4 3 2 1

Keep up with New Holland Publishers:

 NewHollandPublishers

 @newhollandpublishers